AF696753

The Rascal's Guide to Real Estate

By the same author:
The Coming New Zealand Property Boom (1978)
The Property Boom (1981)
Lost Property (first edition 1994)
Lost Property (updated edition 2001)

The Rascal's Guide to Real Estate

Olly Newland

EMPOWER LEADERS PUBLISHING
NEW ZEALAND

To my wife and children and to the memory of my much-loved father, mother, and mother-in-law. Over the decades they collectively shook their heads in disbelief. What had they done to deserve this?

© 2002 Olly Newland & Stellaview Ltd.
All rights reserved.

"The Rascal's Guide" is a registered trademark of Empower Leaders Publishing Ltd.

Contributing editor: Peter Aranyi
Production by Roger Steele at Steele Roberts Ltd
Cover design by Jon Evans, Aotea News
Author photo by Phil Doyle, *Sunday Star-Times*
Printed in New Zealand

Newland, Olly
The Rascal's Guide to Real Estate / Olly Newland,
contributing editor Peter Aranyi
1. Real estate investment. 2. Personal finance.
ISBN 0-9582307-1-4

EMPOWER LEADERS™

Empower Leaders Publishing Ltd
PO Box 39-115 Howick, Auckland, New Zealand
in association with Empower Education Ltd
+64 9 535 2415 • www.EmpowerEducation.com

Contents

PREFACE

Writing this book nearly drove me bonkers. Not because it was so hard, but because there is so much to tell I didn't know where to begin.

There are many books on the market on property investment (and I have written three of them). This book aims to fill an important gap others have not yet covered. That gap is how to deal in property in the Real World.

Theory is one thing. Practice is another.

Most other publications, as good as they may be, are how-to books. They may be factually correct, but just try to put their advice into action. That's a different story.

This book will teach you the techniques, tricks of the trade, and traps for the unwary I've learned over more than forty years as a property investor.

I bought my first property when I was 21. It was a section on the side of a cliff in West Auckland — and the race was on between me and the mountain goats as to who would get there first. I lost. Why I bought it, I have no idea. It was just something you did in those days. It cost me £300 — the equivalent of a year's salary.

Six months later there was a totally unexpected knock on the door. There stood Mr Ah Chong, market gardener of West Auckland standing only 4 feet 10 inches in his socks provided the sun was shining.

He just happened to own the land next door to my section.

"Please Mr Newland," he said, bowing low, "I would like to buy your section."

"How much?" I asked.

"Six hundred pounds," he replied.

That's how it all started.

Without any planning whatsoever I had made a profit of £300 — equal to a year's salary — and without lifting a finger.

Everyone said it was immoral to make such a profit.

Property speculation was evil, they said. The only 'real' money was that earned with your hands and the sweat of your brow. Such deals would attack the fibre of society and bring harm to children, old ladies, and the infirm. Still others said I would never get to heaven, and that at the very least, I should donate the profits to worthy causes and thus bring everlasting blessings on my head.

"Give it back to Society!" was the cry.

"Give it to the Poor and Needy!"

"Sod that for a lark!" I said. (For I was one of the Poor and Needy.)

Eyes bulging, and pocketing the profit, I reluctantly forced myself to carry on for another forty years.

I could not have written this book had it not been for the many wonderful people who helped, encouraged, criticised or just plain lambasted me over the decades. The real estate agents who wasted so much time for the occasional reward, the lawyers who tore their hair out as I blundered through legal minefields, the accountants who never could make head nor tail of the numbers, the enemies I unwittingly created and the friends that I treasured. And of course we mustn't forget the bankers who, bless them, are eaten up with envy at the very thought of a property investor making a few dollars.

There have been so many names and faces over the past forty years that it would be impossible to mention them all. So, rather than offend any of them I shall avoid the task all together.

However, this preface would not be complete without mentioning Peter Aranyi of Empower Education and his good lady wife Pearl Sidwell. It was Peter's constant encouragement that made me finish this book.

Thanks, Peter.

You'll be hearing from my lawyers in the morning.

Olly Newland
Auckland
September 2002

1.

Introduction: To start, first you have to stop

So you want to be a big time property investor? Own scores of properties, have hundreds of tenants. Drive down any street and say, "I own that one."

Well that's all very interesting. Unfortunately the only way you are going to achieve this is to *do nothing*.

Doing nothing is the great secret of the property business.

If you are serious about investing in property, remember it only takes one good deal to change your life.

The problem with our income generating system is that everyone (with the exception of those with wealthy parents) must get up every day five or six days a week and work from dusk to dawn at some job for a fixed payment. Whether it be an hourly rate or an annual salary, it's all the same.

Your maximum possible earnings are limited to the hours you spend on the job. If your wage rate is $20 per hour then the most you can sensibly earn is $800 per week (less tax). That's your life forever, and all you can do is fit your whole life into that $800.

Spare time, hobbies, family and friends, must all be squeezed into the hours left over. Not to mention sleep and play. All spending must fit into that $800.

It's no wonder that gambling, Lotto, and betting on the horses are such a craze. The long odds at least offer dreams if nothing else.

If you have a fixed wage you are effectively a slave.

If you do not work, you starve.

End of story.

To be a successful property investor you must be able to stop and think totally uninterrupted for hours, days or even weeks. Friends can never understand me when I lie under a tree with a loaf of bread, a book, a piece of cheese and seemingly half asleep. They are mystified when I tell them that I am "working" — but it's true.

Property deals must be dreamt up. An investment or speculation has to be thought over carefully, the odds weighed, the approach calculated, the risks evaluated — not to mention the financing and all the advice that has to be absorbed and understood.

Buying a property is not something that can be rushed.

Buy in haste — regret at leisure. That's my motto.

Not only does every deal have to be thought over, it takes much time to even find the deal in the first place. Bargains, or even plain good deals do not fall from Heaven. They are not waiting on every corner. They have to be hunted out if you are very lucky. Usually they have to be created.

And all this takes time.

There is very little hope for the investor who decides on some wet Sunday afternoon to go to a few open homes or answer a few advertisements, find a 'steal' and make millions.

Good deals come up at any time, without notice, and if you want to be successful, you have to be there, right then and there, to close the deal.

Most deals come through real estate agents. It's no use being told of a good deal by an agent and saying that you are busy and will look at it on the weekend.

Agents have books full of property investors who are available on call and who will decide in a flash whether they are in or out. You haven't a chance against that unless you are sitting under that tree waiting, ready to act.

Now, most of you reading this will probably be having the dry horrors right now. The thought of hanging around for days, weeks or months with nothing happening is too horrible to contemplate.

Worse still, there is no income while you wait. For many, this is too hard.

What I have found is that many who are determined to make property investment a serious part of their lives, take on careers that allow them the freedom to jump when asked.

Many investors I know are taxi drivers, real estate agents, commission salesmen ('salespersons' in the laughable PC of our times) or self-employed in some capacity, which gives them income and that important freedom at the same time.

Some send their spouses out to work (now that's a good idea!) so that there is at least some money coming in to feed the chooks.

Your spouse works, while you lie under the tree, thinking, thinking, thinking. The idea is very attractive.

And remember, it only needs one good deal in a lifetime to make all the difference. Over a year it could mean you are doing nothing for 364 days just waiting for that one day that will change things forever.

Now that you have all this free time, you can do some other things to pass the lonely hours. If lying under the tree gets boring, enlarge your knowledge in different ways.

For instance:

(1) Read every advertisement in the papers, or in real estate offices

(2) Visit every open house, everywhere

(3) Reply to all advertisements that have the slightest interest to you

(4) Talk to valuers and get their opinions on what the market is doing

(5) Join the local Property Investors Association

(6) Subscribe to every publication that deals with investment

(7) Make dumb offers with no hope of success just to get the experience (The agents will hate you … tough luck.)

(8) Get every book on the subject and read them

(9) Go to seminars (see www.EmpowerEducation.com)

(10) You can even do a university degree in property investment (in my opinion, the propeller-heads that complete the course still know nothing — it's experience that counts)

(11) Surf the net and research all countries, including New Zealand, for information.

It will take a while and the subject looks daunting and complicated. It is therefore better to concentrate on what you think you are interested in (doing up houses, buying and selling, commercial properties, developing etc). Indeed, you are best served by learning all about one specialised area, or one suburb, or one particular type of investment and getting to know it thoroughly.

In this manner you will become an expert very quickly in a niche market area and can make instant decisions when the opportunity arises.

Getting used to this type of lifestyle is not easy. You must be prepared for some of the downside effects that will come, as sure as God made Little Green Apples.

These are:

(a) An erratic income to say the least. Best to have a small nest egg put aside or someone who is working and keeping you. Bear in mind it may be months before a cent rolls in. When a deal does come off, the results can be very rewarding indeed, far exceeding anything an hourly rate could produce.

(b) The cost of living is expensive under any circumstances and it can be a big strain (if not the biggest strain). It might be a better idea if you live in a house you are doing up for resale. It then makes everything very sensible and rewarding. It also saves you a packet and the results may be tax free as well. Try it!

(c) Being a property investor, no matter how modest, brings out the worst in some people. Many of your friends and acquaintances can become quite jealous of your supposed 'riches', assuming that being a landlord automatically makes you wealthy. The best course to take is to keep private about your affairs and tell no one unless you have to.

Get plenty of hobbies to keep you active. Watching TV endlessly is not a good idea, nor is getting drunk. You must stay active doing something. (Exception: sitting under a tree, thinking.)

The property game can be lonely at times. You will meet some weird people in strange situations from time to time. Do not give in. The rewards are worth it.

2.

Know the difference between *speculating* and *investing*

There are basically two types of property person:

(a) The property investor

and

(b) The property speculator.

The approaches to both activities are quite different. The budding property investor had better decide which camp he or she really belongs in.

Of course, there is no reason someone shouldn't be in both camps, taking on each role on a deal-by-deal basis. That's fine, but experience has shown me that people usually feel the most comfortable being primarily one or the other — and get upset when the two merge.

We had better define more clearly the difference between investors and speculators.

Investors are by definition the more conservative lot, and the more dull and boring as well. Investors buy a property, whether it be a house, flat or block of shops, with the prime purpose of deriving an income stream from it.

Investors are recognised by the fact that they can be seen spending long hours poring over the numbers, adding up, subtracting, and generally making fools of themselves. They are always trying to figure out if only one more dollar could be squeezed out somewhere. They will frequently throw a hissy fit if a tenant is one day late with the rent, or heaven forbid, fails to sweep the pavement before 3pm each Friday.

I pity these poor people. Not for them the stomach-churning tension of tenants who abscond right on Christmas Eve. Nor the sweaty shakes when bills are due and there is nothing in the bank (or even on the horizon). Nor will they know the chilling sight of a vast and echoing empty shop or office that nobody wants, even if it were to be given away free.

On this subject I can talk with some authority. You see, I am one of those investors and consider myself very fortunate. Being labelled "dull and boring" is a Badge of Honour indeed.

For twenty years or more I was an out-and-out speculator. Everything I purchased was back on the market the next day plus a healthy mark-up. That's fine and dandy but the realities of the marketplace dictated the result. For some reason, many properties I bought with the intention to immediately 'flick on' became 'saleproof' straight after they were purchased.

By force I became an investor, living month after month and year after year with my 'flick' which nobody wanted. It meant having to pay the outgoings, dealing with (and dealing to) the tenants, getting toilets unblocked, cleaning off graffiti, and even, (horror of horrors) dealing with the pointy heads in the various City Councils.

I remember one particular deal a long time ago where a development company was feeling the heat and offered me a large site in central

Auckland with an old four-storey, mostly empty, building on it. There was one tenant paying peanuts occupying half the ground floor — but with a long lease.

The building was so crummy that it would have fallen down if it were not for the buildings either side. My research told me that the site, minus the building, was worth at least $800,000 and I was amazed when I bought it for $500,000. This was going to be a killing!

Soon after settlement the truth hit home. It would cost at least half a million to demolish the building, plus another half a million to buy the tenant out of their lease. So much for due diligence on my part!

So, I was forced to become an unwilling long-term investor. The horror stories that I had trying to get any sort of income out of the property would fill several books.

It took twelve years before I sold the property — but it was finally worth it.

The sale price? A cool $2 million cash. The year? 1987. And what did I do with the money? Stuck it all into the sharemarket. Brilliant!!

The big advantage of investing (as opposed to speculating) is that you will have a good idea what your cash flow will be the moment you set eyes on the property. While it is true that there will always be some uncertainty, the basic arithmetic should be easy to work out. You take the rental income, deduct any expenses not recoverable from the tenant, less borrowing costs if you have a mortgage, and the change left over is what should be in the bank.

What is less easy to forecast is where interest rates may go, whether the tenant will renew their lease, or even if the tenant survives at all. Many a time tenants go broke and all the leases and promises will not help in the slightest.

It can be of some comfort to have Personal Guarantees (PGs) from tenants, but again, if they have no money, what use is it? Another comfort is to fix the interest rate on borrowings for as many years ahead as possible so as to increase certainty.

Again, because of Murphy's Law, the day after you fix the mortgage, interest rates go down. (And refinancing can be expensive.)

One of the biggest traps investors can fall into is to assume that a 3 plus 3 plus 3 year lease is a 9 year lease. It is not. It is a three year lease with the tenant having the sole right to renew or leave the premises at their option every three years.

Another trap for beginners is not to calculate exactly what the tenant does and does not pay for. Frequently because some leases can be years old and outdated, the tenant does not pay for water, installing meters, cleaning (even if it's their own dirt), full insurance cover, body corporate fees, management costs, rates increases, lawyers and valuers fees, warrants of fitness, and making good on vacating, to name but a few.

These can eat into any income and effectively reduce it to a very low level, turning what appears to be a good investment into a nightmare.

Property speculators are a completely different breed from investors. While speculators are fully aware of all the ups and downs of pure investment, that is not their aim.

The aim of the speculator is to buy low and sell high in the shortest possible time. In other words, they are *gamblers*.

Not for them the vagaries of leases, tenants and costs. Their goal is to turn a deal over and make a profit on the way. All the rest is far less important.

Speculators are prepared to carry huge losses in hard cash, just to make an even bigger profit. Timing is everything. If they judge right, they make a killing. If they judge wrong, it's down the gurgler.

Let me give you a couple of examples about which I have first-hand knowledge.

A friend of mine has a large old building in the city which he had owned for years. Out of the blue came a gentleman claiming to represent an Asian Consortium looking to amass a land bank on which to erect a hotel. My friend was offered a very healthy price with a down payment of $500,000 to seal the bargain. Excellent.

The speculator went on to similarly buy up at least five other adjoining sites, paying substantial deposits on all of them totalling around $2 million, with a total purchase price of around $25 million.

Then came the Asian Financial Crisis of the late '90s.

It turned out that the speculator had used his own money to make the down payments based on the promises of the Asian buyers. With the best will in the world the Asian buyers could not pay.

The speculator appealed to my friend and the other sellers for a refund of his money. Fat chance! Worse still, my friend had committed himself to yet another deal in the sure and certain hope that his deal would go through. Other vendors had done likewise. What a mess.

After months of stress, heart attacks, and tension, my friend just dug himself out, keeping the deposit, but paying substantial costs and expenses. Others, sadly, were not so lucky.

The speculator went broke, ending up in an institution. Several of the vendors who had on-purchased were cleaned out, losing everything. The 'sold' sites remain untouched to this day.

Admittedly, this was an extreme example that never made the papers. Every day, on a much smaller scale, speculators are beavering away hoping to beat the odds. Some buy houses and flats, clean them up and sell them for a profit. That's speculating. Some buy rundown commercial properties, hoping to sort out the tenants, clean up the property, thereby enhance the value and sell for a profit.

Developers, whether they build cheap home units at $100,000 a pop, or massive shopping malls for millions, are all speculators.

One rule to remember: If you are offered a profit, seriously consider taking it — whether you are an investor or a speculator.

Nobody has ever gone broke making a profit.

3.

Multiplicity is a good thing

Whenever considering your investment portfolio, don't overlook one basic rule: *Spread the Risk.*

It's all very well chasing after lower mortgage interest rates, better insurances, profits and capital gain — but all these will count for nothing if you have fallen into the trap of having one major exposure to the market with nothing to cover it.

Time and again I have seen property investors plunge all their hard-earned savings into a property, using up all their cash reserves in the process, to have it all turn to custard when the tenant disappears or some other trouble erupts.

It doesn't matter if we are talking about a small one-bedroom flat or a $20 million tower block in the city centre, the rules are the same.

Multiple tenancies and multiple properties

Spread the risk by having multiple tenancies and multiple properties.

In other words, if you have (say) $100,000 to invest in residential property, you will be far better off to buy five houses using $20,000 deposit on each than one grand residential investment of $500,000.

Admittedly, residential property is not likely to stay empty for long, but your room to manoeuvre is very limited with only one investment.

Furthermore, should the need arise for cash, it is easier selling with multiple investments. You can sell off one property and keep the rest. This is far easier to achieve and will not rock the boat to the same extent.

Likewise, when investing in residential property, it is wiser to buy a block of two or more flats. If one becomes empty for any reason the other will at least provide some cash flow while you sort matters out.

Consider this as well: Buying just one flat in a larger block is not the best idea. You may have good control of your tenant and ensure the flat is kept tidy at all times, but have you any control over the others?

I learnt that lesson the hard way when in a moment of temporary insanity I bought a small unit in a block of four. What I did not realize was that the other three were owned by an overseas investor who had no direct interest in managing his flats. He left that to the tender mercies of his teenage son who resided here.

As is well known, the successful management of residential tenants is akin to running an overcrowded abattoir during an earthquake. Not for the fainthearted or inexperienced.

In my case, the other three flats were infested with bands of street kids, drunken hooligans, and other cave dwellers who emerged at night to terrorise the neighbourhood.

Naturally, I had seen my investment during the day and had assumed that the peacefulness was part and parcel of the whole block. Not so. The peacefulness was due to the other inhabitants sleeping off their hangovers during daylight hours.

Another lesson: View your investment in daylight and at night before putting in the offer.

Likewise with location. Everyone knows that location is one of the key factors in attaining a good return from a property, whether it be rental or capital growth.

Purchasing just one property restricts the investor greatly. Things can and do go wrong. A good location today may become a bad one tomorrow. A zoning change, a development next door, or a street widening to name but a few can turn a brilliant investment into an OPT.*

And the opposite is equally true. I once owned a property in a street that was, in effect, a motorway. Through traffic roared past night and day. A good renter, and sound — but that was all. Lo and behold, out of the blue the City Council advised all the owners in the street that they were closing the street off and turning it into a cul-de-sac. Values increased overnight by 25%.

Commercial property (factories, shops, offices, etc) is much more vulnerable to vacancy factors and it is not unusual for commercial space to lie empty for months and sometimes for years.

Anyone considering investment into commercial had better realise that it is vital to have multiple tenancies (billionaires excepted) — at least two tenants (preferably more) per building, and where the leases are not riding in tandem. This simple precaution may well save your neck (not to mention your frazzled bank manager). The likelihood that all the tenants vacate at same time is far more remote.

The downside with multiple tenancies is the management. Of course it is easier to have one tenant and one lease in one building. Multiple tenancies mean that management becomes more and more difficult the more tenants you have. But it's worth it. Many an investor has gone down the drain because the tenant either left or went broke. Either way, the result is an empty building and misery all round.

Multiple use

One issue frequently overlooked in commercial property is the multiple-use factor.

Commercial property should not be too specialized. Frequently tenants need or build special features required for their line of business

*OPT = Over-priced turkey

but which are useless for anyone else.

When the tenant moves out or goes broke, the landlord has to face the double horror of finding a new tenant and spending a fortune as well rebuilding or removing the special structures.

The most vivid experience I had in this regard was a factory offered to me with an extraordinarily high yield and solid tenant. On inspection, I found this large factory filled with workers hammering and banging away around the clock three shifts a day.

The huge spaces within were filled with steaming cauldrons, bubbling tanks, pipes hissing and roaring, water and power cables running everywhere. Overhead and on the floor machines buzzed and roared. It looked like a scene out of Dante's *Inferno*. The business was an electroplating and sheet metal factory — and a very successful one at that.

This was too good to be true. Dollar signs swam before my eyes. I got ready to put in an unconditional offer and fast! There were other investors snooping around.

My valuer put me right. He refused to value the property, cautioned me in writing against it, and in particular warned me of the pollution all around the site. Some day, someone would have to clean it all up. It would cost them hundreds of thousands of dollars to put right. Sorry, not me.

Multiple sources of finance

Multiple sources of finance are another wise precaution.

Too often I see investors use one bank for all their dealing, both private and business. Lenders frequently ask that all your business be put through them in return for better facilities or lower charges. This is all well and good. It seems to make sense to have your home mortgage, business overdraft, personal overdraft, car, hire purchases, credit cards and deposits all at one bank.

That is until something goes wrong. Then it is too late. Many an innocent has been badly mauled when something goes awry with even only part of one's private or business life. I've seen people who defaulted on their hire purchase, only to find out that a default in that area created an automatic default through the lot. The lender can then grab the bag (and believe me, they will!) Everything can go down the drain including bank deposits offset against debt.

It is wiser to borrow from different lenders. Lender A on the home, Lender B on the business, deposits with another bank and so forth. Then in case of problems, only a part of what you have worked so hard for is grabbed. Not very nice, but better than the lot disappearing.

You can go even further by having your home in a Trust, your business owned by one company, your cars owned by another and thus put up perfectly legal barriers should trouble arise.

Although multiple anythings do complicate matters and create management bottlenecks, in the long run, it is a simpler provision than trying to sort out a mess afterwards. Investment is tricky at the best of times. If you are making good profits then matters will look after themselves. It's only when things go wrong that you find out it's too late.

Multiple entities and multiple bank accounts

To become really savvy, it is a good idea to operate separate accounts for every property. Indeed a separate company or Trust for every property or more practically, *type* of property.

So you can have company XYZ for flats, company ABC for houses, company DEF for buying and selling and so on. (See the chapter on tax for more detail.) With different accounts and different entities and different banks it can become an accountant's nightmare — but it is all done in the name of protecting your assets as much as possible.

Avoid personal guarantees wherever possible

The fly in the ointment comes when the lenders insist on guarantees either personal or between or from companies or Trusts. In this way, all the fire-walls so installed are circumvented. *Avoid these as much as possible.* Even be willing to pay a higher rate of interest (within reason) if that helps. At all costs keep your private assets (e.g. your home or bank deposits) completely out of the picture.

Overdrafts

When it comes to dealing with trading banks it is a good idea to keep any overdrafts as small as possible. This means that you may not have to give security. It also means that every little company or Trust can have its own overdraft, which can be handy. Should you have ten entities and an overdraft of $5000 for each you get effectively an overdraft of $50,000 unsecured.

The problem with overdrafts is that they can be called up instantaneously, which can be awkward in the extreme. A mortgage or other such instrument takes longer to call up and gives you much more time to straighten out any problems. In the end, of course, you have to pay, even if it's on the courthouse steps.

Time brings multiple opportunities so if nothing else, buy time.

Multiple professionals

My final advice when it comes to multiples of anything is to consider multiple solicitors, accountants, valuers and other like professions. Take solicitors, for instance. Some are very good in conveyancing work, but not too good on litigation. (You will have plenty of that, believe me!) It is worth considering having a solicitor for your private affairs (home, family, wills etc) and another entirely different solicitor for conveyancing. This way nobody knows all your business if you like to be private.

Likewise it pays to use several valuers. At any given time a property can have multiple values. Valuing is not an exact science. One valuer may put $200,000 on a property and another $220,000, yet both could argue successfully that they are right.

If you are trying for a loan of 75% of valuation the difference in the hand would be $15,000 more with the higher value. This could make or break a deal.

4.

Always look for Blue Sky deals

One of the most frequent errors budding property investors make is to become so besotted by a prospective property purchase that they forget the Blue Sky aspect.

Yet this is probably more important than anything else. The Blue Sky is that monetary value that can be added to a property investment with the minimum effort and expense and providing the maximum increase in capital gain in the shortest possible time. (In other words, the biggest bang for the bucks.)

Blue Sky is attained in the following ways:

(1) Buying well under market value

(2) Improving the property

(3) Knowing something special about the property or its neighbourhood

(4) Selling on easy terms

(5) Most important: buying in an *area* that allows for Blue Sky.

Buying under market

At any one time a property can have several different values, all of which are legitimate at one and the same time.

These values depend on the circumstances under which the property is sold or valued.

For instance a different price (viz. value) for the same property can be seen with:

(a) Government Valuation (GV) or Council Valuation (CV)

(b) Trustee valuations by valuers

(c) Market valuations by real estate agents or valuers

(d) Fire sale values in cases of emergency

(e) Easy terms values.

All these circumstances can alter a price dramatically. I once had dealings with a property which had a Trustee valuation of $495,000 but was sold for $390,000 and then on-sold for $460,000 and had a CV of $525,000 — all within the space of three months. Same house, same land, same market, but what a difference in price!

How did this come about? Simple. The house was sold at $390,000 by a vendor who was going under and needed to get out fast. He traded it to a developer who couldn't really afford to hang on to it and dumped it at cost. The buyer (whom I know very well — ahem!) bought it, mowed the lawns and resold it for $460,000. This was still a bargain for the purchaser as it had a trustee valuation of $495,000 all the while.

This was an easy example of recognising Blue Sky when it hits you in the face. Mind you, not all are as easy as that, so don't get carried away. Most are far more subtle.

Remember that 95% of buyers and sellers don't have to sell or buy. They would love to, indeed they may yearn for a sale or a purchase. They may toss and turn all night wishing and hoping but in the end, when push comes to shove, they don't *have* to.

The three Ds of real estate

It is in the last 5% that the Blue Sky can be found. This 5% arises almost always through pressure from the three Ds of real estate:

Death

Divorce, and

D

Death

Some ... ates. Usually the benefici... cash that they will sell a pr... l chew gum at the same ti... are a number of benefici... ı, and so becomes virtually...

Divorce

Divorce ... en a couple split up, the h... city for a month. In these ... n to (a) get away from eac... as possible, that either is ... ent at any price. Some of ... cumstances.

I parti... perty was for sale due to a s... o the house with the childr... wer to sell but as no one co... ere. Never fear. I knocked ... e of which was usefully tw... oughly inspected the grounds and much of the interior in this manner. The husband also gave me photos in his possession, all of which convinced me that the property was sound and in good decorative order. The rest was history and a good deal was the inevitable outcome.

1921
1921
55GSJ1000XU2
Title THE RASCAL S GUIDE TO REAL ESTAT
Condition Good
Location Room A Bay 3 Item 1921
Description Paperback.
Source Incoming
SKU 55GSJ1000XU2
ASIN 0958230714
Code 9780958230711
Employee lydia
Date Added 11/29/2022 3:08:41 PM

De Bank

Financial pressure is second only to marriage split ups. Most people overreact when the bank comes a-knocking. This is understandable considering the lamentable history of banks and their propensity to knee-jerk if given the slightest opportunity. When trouble looms from this quarter, many vendors panic to such an extent that they sell up and give their properties away just to get relief from the pressure. This is erroneous of course, as all banks will assist if approached. They don't want to be seen throwing people out of their homes too readily, otherwise no one would borrow from them. However, this doesn't alter the fact that people do panic and great bargains can be obtained in this manner.

This is especially so at mortgagee sales where the bank is selling a property under its power of sale. At a mortgagee sale the bank can only recover what is owed and no more. In many cases what is owed is much less than the property is worth (unbelievable as it may seem) so thundering bargains are frequent.

Even better still, these sales are not counted when valuers do their sums. Valuers can only use figures obtained from sales between willing buyers and sellers, not forced sales.

Invest where there is no upper limit on prices

Another useful way to cash in on Blue Sky is to buy only where there is no limit on prices. Many suburbs have masses of look-alike working class homes (housing working class people.) When you get areas like that it is a fundamental error to think that by buying well and perhaps doing some improvement work that the property will automatically go up in value. Although profits are quite possible, these suburbs have a ceiling for prices so no matter what you do, this ceiling is impossible to break. In other words, if you buy a house at $200,000 in an area where the maximum price is around $250,000 then you have $50,000 at the most in which to fit your profit. That $50,000 has to cover all holding costs, agents' fees, legal expenses, improvement costs and of course, your profit. A simple exercise will show how tight the profit really is and how quickly it can turn into a loss.

The answer is to invest in areas where there is no limit on prices — where $200,000 houses are in the same street as million-dollar properties. Generally these areas are found in the older and more established suburbs. Therefore it is less of a problem to take a cheaper property and, by improving it or by just buying it well, to on-sell it for a profit.

For example, in Auckland working class homes are in the main found in the western or southern suburbs like Te Atatu or Glen Eden or Mangere, and Blue Sky properties are often found in areas such as Parnell, Orakei, Remuera and St Heliers which are in the eastern suburbs. This is of course a sweeping generalisation but the principle is true enough.

Finding Blue Sky in commercial property (shops, offices, factories etc)

The Blue Sky element in commercial property has some nice twists to it. The obvious advantages of location, state of repair, soundness of the tenant can be taken for granted, but there are some more subtle angles as well.

(1) Knowing in advance about major improvements nearby can materially improve the value of a commercial property. For instance, those brave investors who purchased property near the Britomart development in downtown Auckland will be laughing all the way to the bank. (Provided the politicians don't mess it up!) Much of the information an investor needs is already in the public domain — it just needs interpretation.

Prudent investors keep in touch with City Council planners and real estate agents, generally keeping their ears to the ground. In this way they buy ahead of the market, becoming aware of future trends early on in the piece.

(2) Understanding the correct level of commercial rentals is always a useful tool to obtain Blue Sky in a hurry.

Many landlords have little or no idea what the market rental should be for shops, offices or factories. They either ask too little, or forget to keep up with any rent increases over the years. Along comes a wide-awake investor who, with a little enquiry, finds out that a particular commercial property is under-rented. After buying the property for a song, the rents are adjusted and the value shoots up.

What many people often do not appreciate is that the value of commercial property is set by the rental it produces. This is quite unlike residential property where the value is set by one market, and the rental is set by a different market.

In other words, if a commercial property is producing $100,000 rental per annum net, then at a 10% yield its value is $1 million. Increase the rent to $110,000 and the value becomes $1.1 million. You can see in this simple exercise than a mere $10,000 a year rent increase added $100,000 to the wealth of the investor. Not a bad return. The twists come in trying to keep the yield down as low as possible. The lower the yield, the higher the value given a fixed rental return.

The commercial market is a minefield (or gold-mine depending on your point of view) for investors to manipulate rents, yields and values with the aim to not only increase rents but values as well.

This has nothing to do with inflation.

In one experience I purchased a commercial property that was partially empty and producing only $65,000 p.a. The purchase price was $800,000 which reflected the fact that the empty space would get something. Instead of letting the empty portion for the expected rent I let the space out in small bits to various sub-tenants for much higher rentals — small spaces command premium rents. The rental shot up to $115,000 net. My valuer suggested 9% as a yield. You work out its value today. *

* $1,270,000

Blue Sky is an essential element to consider when purchasing any property.

Before signing your life away, check not only the construction, the LIM (Land Information Memorandum) report, a valuation report, finance and rents, but ask yourself one more question:

What will the value of this property be 5, 10 or 15 years from now, without relying on inflation?

If the answer is positive, then buy in confidence.

5.

Real estate agents: their treatment and cure

No matter how hard you try, an inescapable fact of life is that real estate agents play a vital role for property investors. With rare exceptions the underworld of agents festers with intrigue, back-stabbing, exaggeration, bitchiness and downright untruths.

However, it is not my habit to mock the afflicted. Therefore I shall draw the curtain of charity over their foibles. Instead, I will tell you how to use them to best advantage.

It is no use trying to avoid them. They have cornered the market. Sooner or later you will read an advertisement or see a sign on a property compelling you to pick up the phone and do something. Even the internet has its limitations. Nothing beats actually touching and feeling and (frequently) smelling the real thing.

First and foremost, when dealing with agents tell them *nothing* about yourself or your financial situation. Keep your mouth shut.

Just listen, nod quietly, and let your eyes glaze over during the customary torrent of verbiage.

The reason for keeping quiet is simple. If you tell an agent that you are a novice, know nothing about investment or property, and you are just starting to learn out of a book, they will either tuck you into an OPT (see previous chapter) or look heavenwards while moving quickly out of range.

By all means, use the internet, open homes and advertisements in general to get a feel for what you might want, but you can only dream for so long. Eventually you will have to go into the real world and take action.

Open homes

The quickest way to learn is to go to all the open homes possible. This is a popular weekend pastime for thousands of people who love perving at other people's homes without the slightest intention of buying anything.

The rules are simple:

For Buyers

(1) Wear slip-on shoes. Every open home requires that shoes be removed. It becomes positively tiresome to be tying and untying shoelaces or pulling off boots ten times an hour. I have a wonderful set of 'brothel creepers' especially for the purpose. They are so garish they are never confused in the jumble of shoes found at every front door of an open home.

(2) When inside you will be asked for your name and phone number. Give your mother's maiden name and your bank manager's phone number. Let them be bothered by pesky agents.

(3) When looking about, mumble *sotto voce* how expensive the place is, how badly it compares with the one you saw down the road (even if it was a broken down chicken coop), how everything

needs repainting and fixing etc. This is not idle. Real estate agents are born with ears that can hear through six foot cavity block walls against prevailing winds while the stereo is playing the *Warsaw Concerto.*

Agents love to hear 'feedback' to relate to the seller. OK. So give them feedback that suits your purpose. Indeed, many agents at open homes ask you what *you* think the property is worth. Give them a ridiculously low figure. It all helps.

(4) Look carefully at the finish of the surfaces and the quality of the fittings. Everything looks good when it's new. Yet the quality might be that of a sewage worker's hut in outer Mongolia. Learn to tell the difference.

(5) Look into the cupboard spaces carefully. Most places have woefully inadequate cupboard space and it's easily overlooked. Be careful. You can get into bother poking around.

I recall going to an open home once and prying into all sorts of nooks and crannies to see what I could see. I was intrigued to find a door high up in the attic which seemed heavily locked. Strange? Why did it have black polythene taped over its surface, and a feeling, indeed an *odour* of mustiness wafting from behind? No matter how hard I tried, I could not pull open the door. There is nothing like a challenge. When nobody was looking, I found a trowel, and huffing and puffing I jemmied the door open. (It was an open home after all, I thought. I was entitled to see everything.)

The agent's screams hit me at force nine as she appeared on the scene just as the door sprung its hinges. On the other side lay a large brightly lit room, with hundreds of healthy marijuana plants all in rows, nicely bathed with heat lamps and a fine mist of water. In a twinkling a crowd had gathered and everyone else in the house was looking in. The agent began to have hysterics.

Onlookers took bets as to the value of the crop. Children pointed with tremulous fingers.

"What's that, Mummy?" they asked, their eyes getting wider by the minute. "Hush, darling," their mother said, clapping a hand over her children's mouths. "It's spinach which makes you grow up big and strong."

The property was withdrawn from the market the next day and I didn't answer the phone for a week.

(6) When leaving, take away all the brochures, pamphlets and titles you can to remind you of what you have seen. (Also try to take away better shoes than those you came with. You never know your luck.)

For Sellers

Selling by way of an open home is stressful to say the least. Most people would rather eat a plateful of live centipedes than go through the experience more than once. However, it is something that often has to be done, and here are some basic rules:

(1) Give your property a thorough spring clean. It is exhausting work (for somebody) but must be done. The sight of scum rings in the bath or rancid milk containers on the kitchen bench does nothing to enhance your chances.

(2) Empty the house of all clutter. Every room must be stripped to the bare essentials. Toys, magazines, books, prams, bottles, after shave, hair curlers, nick-nacks of every sort must be boxed and stored.

(3) Alternatively, if clutter is your thing, then do a proper job of it and fill the place up to the ceilings with collectables.

I once went through an open home which sat right by the motorway. The traffic din shook the house and its occupants to the foundations. However, every room in the house was filled with the most incredible junk I have ever seen. The hallway was filled with books, a stuffed alligator, brass shell cases, flags of various nations, trophy deer heads (2), Victorian kerosene lights, and a penny farthing bicycle.

Each bedroom overflowed with a *mélange* of 19th century nick-nacks and drapery. There were dead birds in glass cases, old fashioned prams, kitchen pots, jelly moulds and pewter plates. In dark corners stood replica suits of armour, old rifles and swords, telescopes on stands, and globes of the world.

The kitchen and bathroom were no better, with Victorian flowered toilets, wash basins and ewers, florid towels and curtains, innumerable copper pans and vast clay pots which may have contained human mummies for all I knew. The garden was also packed. Concrete gnomes, pink flamingos, a World War 1 field cannon(!), a wishing well, wooden benches, flower beds and rustic wheelbarrows.

It was all very clever. The owners knew that the house on its own with the motorway at the back fence would never sell. By raiding the antique and junk shops they cunningly diverted attention from their major drawback and replaced it with something much more interesting — and they could take it all away later (to sell, presumably).

The house sold within a week. Moral: If your property has a serious drawback emphasise a big feature elsewhere.

(4) It's an old trick but it works: Just before the open home reheat or bake some bread and brew some fresh coffee (the agents will eat and drink them, never fear). The aroma drives people crazy.

(5) All smelly odours (dog, cat, cigarettes) must be removed. A total wash down and carpet shampoo may be absolutely essential.

(6) Make sure the garden is neat and tidy, rubbish removed, hedges cut, lawns mowed.

(7) Touch up all chipped paint and repair all *visible* faults (see later chapters on house renovation).

(8) Ask all your friends to visit the property during the open home times. The bigger the crowd the more people get interested.

(9) Get a valuation done on the property, either from a registered valuer or from the agents. If the figure is in your favour, have copies available ready to be dished out when the need arises. Something in writing is a very useful weapon when the heavy breathing starts.

Agents: tactics & terms

Right from the beginning, if you are thinking about making an offer, stay in charge of the situation. It's your offer. You dictate what is written up. Don't be bullied by the agent and agree to something you are not happy with. Many agents will write up an agreement and positively embarrass you with the terms. Naturally, their job is to tie you up as tightly as possible.

From the beginning, think about into whose name you are buying the property. If you are not sure add the words "or nominee" after your name and sort it out later. (See chapter on tax and legal structures.)

Ensure that the legal description of the property is 100% correct. (Not the street address, that can vary over time). Many a deal has come unstuck because of one number or letter omitted from the legal description.

Do not hand over *any* deposit money until the deal is unconditional. If there is a dispute, your deposit will stay locked up in the agent's Trust Account forever and a day.

Ensure you are buying the land as well as the house (viz. it is not leasehold land). That bargain price may be simply due to the property being leasehold and is a trap for the beginner.

A favourite trick of agents is the 'One, Two, Three,' try-out. They take you on a tour of what is for sale in your price range. First they take you to something that is ghastly and hopelessly overpriced. Then they take you to something which is even worse, to really depress you. Then they take you to the one they really want you to see. Naturally, you fall for that one as it's so much superior.

Easy as pie.

Deal done.

Don't fall for it.

Real estate advertisements

Translating agents' advertisements is an art form in itself. Bear in mind that advertisements are often an admission of failure. By the time agents get a property advertised in the paper (or on the Net) they would have already flogged it around to their regular buyers waiting in the wings — who've all turned it down!

This doesn't mean you will miss out on a good deal, but it does show that good deals are made, not advertised. No one intends to sell their property too cheaply. You *create* a good deal by negotiation — and to do that, you must be there in person working with the agent. Being a 'Wet Sunday' investor is a waste of everyone's time (including yours).

Therefore, all the hype you read about *Bargain, Bargain, Bargain!* is just that — hype. Don't believe it.

A guide to reading advertisements

"Five minutes from beach"

> Translation: If you own an Aston Martin V8 supercharged hand-made sports car, then it's just possible on a dark night to get to the beach in five minutes probably collecting a dozen tickets for dangerous driving on the way.

"Magnificent views"

> Translation: By standing on tiptoes on a stack of books and a tall chair and leaning out of the attic window using a shaving mirror on a stick you just might see a cup of water on a clear day.

"Elevated views" (sometimes known as "Standing Proud")

Translation: Don't bother looking unless you have spent five years training in the Himalayas and own a four-wheel drive with wire rope winch front and back.

"Requires TLC"

Translation: This place is a Dog. It will need an army of tradesmen and a million dollars before it comes right — if at all.

"Cosy living"

Translation: The rooms are so small when you smile your cheeks touch the opposite walls.

"On bus route"

Translation: There's no garage.

"Garden is a child's dream"

Translation: The garden is so overgrown that it's been declared a wild life sanctuary — and strange things rustle in the undergrowth.

"Rustic charm"

Translation: All the paint has fallen off the walls and the plumbing doesn't work.

"Secluded private section"

Translation: Full training in hang gliding would be an asset (see "elevated views" above).

"Open plan living"

Translation: There's only one decent room.

In all seriousness, far and away most deals are done through real estate agents. Their main advantage is that they provide a neutral barrier and, hopefully, some professionalism between you and the buyer or seller as the case may be.

It is not easy to deal directly with buyers and sellers when such large amounts of money are involved (not to mention sometimes highly-charged emotions). This is why private sales only work to a limited degree. The agent acts as a buffer when your 'insultingly' low offer (and as an investor, you *must* offer low) needs to be presented to the vendor.

Commissions

Agents make their living from commissions on sales. The commission is based on a percentage of the sale price and is calculated on a formula the agent should disclose if you ask. But like everything in real estate, it is negotiable! Discuss the commission *before* making or receiving an offer.

As commissions are deregulated, there is nothing to stop you cutting the commission, either before you start or, better still, at the point of signing up. The best time of all to haggle over commission is when the parties are so close that it is only the commission standing in the way.

Don't forget, the agent is as hungry as you are. Strike when the deal is right at the critical point. Nine times out of ten it works — and you save thousands of dollars.

Agents and auctions

Many properties are sold by auction.

In actual fact 99% of vendors would love to sell prior to auction as the preparation and stress leading up to the Big Day are more than most can bear.

Agents use the line that auction tests the true market value (whatever that means) which is bunkum. As each property is unique, and each buyer even more unique, it is virtually impossible to find a consensus from the 'market'.

In reality an auction does more for the agent than it does for the vendor or buyer. It focuses attention on the property and puts some tension in the air. Remember, it is the seller who is paying for all the advertising hype, and this is factored into the price — along with the commission when the property is sold.

The main problem with auctions is that the right buyer may not be in the market during the few weeks the property is achieving its high profile. The buyer may be three months away or even six months away. Take heart. Everything sells in the end.

As an example of the faulty auction process, here's a true story which happened to a good friend of mine. He and his good lady wife owned a superior eastern suburbs home that was worth close to $1 million. The auction process was agreed upon and the agents brought hundreds of potential buyers along. Open homes were arranged, hoardings erected, advertisements inserted in papers and on the Net — all at the seller's expense, of course. Despite people coming back, three or four times in many cases, not one single solitary offer was forthcoming.

Weeks went by, and nothing but endless hordes of lookers. My friend was in despair and his wife close to a nervous breakdown.

Out of the blue, a perfect stranger phoned and asked if they would consider selling their house. He had been in the property ten years previously, having known the previous owner. He had no idea it was then actually on the market, and had not seen any of the advertisements. He came right over and within one hour had bought it. The agents, to their everlasting credit, took a big cut in their commission under the circumstances.

So much for the hype surrounding auctions.

Auction tactics

When auction day arrives you can be certain that whether you are the buyer or seller the agents will bowing and scraping fit to bust. To the seller they will be trying to get the expected price down, and to the buyer exactly the opposite. Considerable pressure will be exerted on both ends by the agents who, despite protests to the contrary, are working entirely for themselves at all times.

If you are the seller, it is essential that you never to give the agent your reserve price at any stage. Indeed, you may change your mind as the auction process goes along — either up or down. Tough on the nerves as it might be, keep your reserve to yourself right up to the fall of the hammer. The auctioneer will ask you if the last bid is enough, then you can decide with a simple nod of the head, yes or no.

If you are a buyer, I strongly recommend that you do not tell the agent that you will be bidding at the auction. You can however, register your interest prior to the auction. This means that if an offer goes in prior to auction you will be contacted and asked to put an offer in as well. By the time of the auction, sort out your price limit and say nothing.

When it comes to limits, be flexible. If a property is worth (say) $300,000 then a few thousand more is of little consequence. There are legions of frustrated buyers wandering around now, forlorn and miserable having lost the property of their dreams for the sake of a few dollars. As has been said before: *Long after the price is paid, the value remains.*

As the bidding starts, keep your hands to your sides until the very last moment. You will be the 'surprise' bidder. Don't worry. The auctioneer will not bring down the hammer without plenty of prior warning.

If you find this all too hard, get your solicitor or somebody with iron nerves to bid for you. (Probably your banker is the best — they have no nerves).

Should you reveal your interest to the agents prior to auction you can be sure that:

(a) they'll hound you day and night to make an offer prior to auction

(b) everything they say should be taken with a grain of salt

(c) on auction day they will be tugging at your sleeve, kissing your backside, and whispering sweet nothings in your ear to increase your offer.

As a seller exactly the same applies. The same tactics, the same unctuous backside kissing, the same pressure, all designed to make you accept an offer that isn't anything like you hoped for.

All but a few auctioneers take 'fly spot' bids at auctions. This creates the impression that there are many bidders fighting for the property when in truth there may be only one — you. It's all a part of the game. So long as you know this beforehand you are forewarned and therefore forearmed.

I had an experience not too long ago with a well-known firm of agents (I recounted this in the updated edition of *Lost Property*, but it bears repeating) who were auctioning off a property which to my mind had potential — provided it was bought cheaply enough.

We all know that real estate agents are as bad as property investors when it comes to hype and exaggeration, but this lot stole the prize. The property was advertised and I duly asked for the information on it, e.g. leases, titles, LIM reports etc. To my surprise, none of the information was available. "Still coming from the accountants," I was told. Not very impressive.

The days and weeks rolled by and the auction date was getting closer and still no information was available. "The accountant is out of the country", "The vendors are elderly," they said, etc.

At the same time, the agents were telling me to put in a pre-auction offer because of the keen interest shown by many prospective purchasers. Now, that was strange. How do the other purchasers make offers with no information?

So I used my noodle. The only information I did have was a rental assessment done by a valuer I knew well. As luck would have it, he knew all the rest about the property and within half an hour I had the lot. Keeping this to myself, I waited and wasn't surprised when the agents finally produced all the information the day before the auction!

By then I had finance arranged, valuations done and attended the auction with some confidence.

Up came my lot. The auction room burst with activity. Faxes buzzed, agents ran around with bits of paper, bids were coming off the walls, off the floor, out of the chandeliers, and from half a dozen mobile phones.

How could this be possible? I kept my hands by my sides.

Finally it was hammered down as sold at just a whisker above my price (which I hadn't revealed of course). That was very odd. I recognised the buyer as an agent of the firm doing the auction.

I stood up to leave. But wait, what was this? Several agents were pulling at my sleeve. "Please come into the office to discuss your under-bid," they begged.

In their terms, the successful bidder had "buggered off." Would I like to buy it at the same price?

I told them what a bunch of twits they were (to put it kindly), trying to fool me — but I did end up buying the property nevertheless.

I also extracted a promise that they would never try that sort of stunt on me again. They promised faithfully. I didn't believe a word of it — not then. Not now.

One final word: When selling a property prior to auction the first offer is usually the best.

Buyers love fresh stock. They can get very excited when something new comes on — especially after having been dragged around innumerable dungers, basket cases, and OPTs.

So, when selling, don't let the first offer go too quickly.

6.

Documentation — Part 1: The paper war

If anything is ever going to trip you up in property investing it will be faulty or poorly thought out documentation.

It is a matter of fact that everything to do with real estate must be in writing. Verbal contracts, handshake deals, deals done on the back of a cigarette packet are all worthless.

Money does strange things to people's minds. Amnesia, double vision, forgery, greed, lies, and errors all become magnified when large sums are at stake. All property deals, even trivial ones, must be in writing, signed by all parties and as clear and unambiguous as possible.

Now this is all well and good but the pitfalls are many. Clever lawyers make a career out of finding errors in written deals so they can poke their snouts into the trough that much deeper.

It is so easy to get into deals.

It is so hard to get out of them.

The documentation must be dead right for your peace of mind or you will pay the consequences. Even then there are no guarantees — but at least give yourself every chance.

Sale and Purchase Agreements

The current edition (as I write this) of the standard form approved by the Real Estate Institute and the Law Society is headed up top right corner 'Seventh edition (2) July 1999.'

Before doing anything else *get yourself a copy and study all the fine print.* (Ask your friendly real estate agent for a copy, or, failing that, contact Empower Education who can make one available for a small fee.)

There is nothing wrong in using the 6th, 5th, or 4th edition if a copy is lying about, but no matter what changes have been made, or conditions inserted or omitted, you will be bound by them.

Filling in the form is an art in itself. With a copy by your side, we can go through the principal clauses step by step.

If you think this is all a waste of time, believe me it is not. The Sale and Purchase Agreement is the only document in the real estate world that is most commonly signed under pressure — either when buying or selling. All other documentation can be studied at leisure. e.g. leases, tenancy agreements, variations, mortgages etc.

Not so the Sale and Purchase Agreement. You will undoubtedly have a real estate agent breathing fire and brimstone over your trembling hands as you try to make sense out of the gobbledegook placed before you. (Not to mention anxious partners, children and relatives putting on the pressure as well.)

Hence, a basic understanding of what is contained in the form is a must.

First page

(1) **The date:** Leave this blank when filling in the form. You will note that on several occasions time limits are given (e.g. 15 days for a LIM report). The date is inserted only when all parties have reached an agreement and signed whether it be conditional or unconditional.

(2) **Vendor:** If you are the seller your name goes in here, but ensure that it is the same name or names as are on the title.

(3) **Purchaser:** If you are the buyer, decide from the outset what name you want the property registered into. If you are not sure, put "or nominee" or "as trustee" after your name. This way you can decide between making the agreement and settlement.

This is also useful if you manage to find another buyer who will purchase from you prior to your settling. The new buyer accepts the nomination (in writing of course) and settles up in your stead. Be warned: if he or she doesn't settle the seller can come back to you for the money!

(4) **Address:** Don't be fooled into thinking that if the address is right then you have bought the right property. Many a time addresses have been changed — especially if sections have been re-surveyed and new addresses were needed. Often too, street names have been changed. The address is a convenience — not a watertight legality.

(5) **Estate:** 'fee simple, leasehold, cross lease, unit title' etc. If nothing is touched here than the property is purchased in 'fee simple' i.e. freehold. (This does ***not*** mean free of debt. It means that you are buying the land plus the buildings.) I make a practice of putting a circle around the actual one so that there is no doubt whatsoever.

(6) **Legal description:** At this point the greatest care must be taken to exactly copy the full legal description from the title on this space. The smallest error can be a disaster — especially if one party or the other has second thoughts.

I had the experience of selling a property which was described as "Unit H" etc on the agreement form. The true legal description was "Part Unit H" and, despite all my lecturing on care and correctness, both the agent and I had missed this minor point.

It wasn't minor, though, to the buyer or his smart-aleck lawyer. To them it was a godsend. The lawyer for the buyer demanded to know where the other 'part' was. If his client was actually buying a 'part' then he expected the other 'part' as well — or a reduction in price as he was losing out on a 'part'. All legal nonsense, of course, but it was a close thing. Many deals have crashed because of errors like this.

There is a disease called Buyer's Remorse (Latin: *lackus monicum gigantus)* which runs rampant through the property world and for which there is no known cure. The symptoms are wailing, gnashing of teeth, and running off to lawyers to try to get out of a deal. Be prepared for it. It is common.

(7) **GST**: Watch this one. Generally speaking, used dwellings have no GST to pay (unless you are a dealer). On the other hand, new houses and apartments carry GST in the price right down to the last nail and screw. To complicate matters, many apartments are sold when new into a Hotel Pool for leasing out. They do not have to pay GST as they are 'going concerns'. The trouble comes when the owner of this gilt edged (hah!) investment wants to take it out of the Hotel Pool (or more likely is tossed out), then GST becomes payable. Many people have bought second-hand apartments thinking they are GST-free when they are not. Somebody has to pay, and there have been some mighty fights over this. The moral therefore, is to ensure you know *exactly* what the GST position is whether you are buying or selling. Check with your lawyer or accountant before signing if in doubt.

(8) **Deposit:** Another trap for the unwary. There is no such thing as a compulsory deposit when making an offer (unless it's an auction). A bottle top, half a boiled chicken or a length of knotted string is just as valid as cash. Mind you, the seller doesn't need to accept that either.

When making an offer to purchase, keep the deposit as small as possible (enough to whet the appetite of the agent). Do not pay it until the offer is unconditional. At this point I can hear a chorus of groans from agents. Agents live for the deposits as they take their commission out of them. Tough luck.

The point is that if you have made an offer with conditions, you do not want a large chunk of your capital tied up in an agent's Trust account. Murphy's Law is alive and well in the real estate world. Often a deal will fall over for reasons outside the contract (which is bad enough). In that case your deposit is retained while you engage in a legal fight that could drag on for months or even years.

In many situations agents get their commission no matter what the fight is over. So you can see why you do not pay until you are quite sure of what you are doing. Better to fight with your money intact.

On the other hand, if you want to make an impact and are sure of your position, then an unconditional contract with a cheque attached is a powerful weapon to get a bargain.

(9) **Possession:** This refers to the date you take the property over. If either you or the other party are flexible then insert the words "on or before" such and such date. The possession date need not be the date you actually pay for the property. You can have a possession date different from the day you settle. However, commonly both occur simultaneously.

(10) **Interest Late Settlement:** This is the amount you can charge (or be charged) if you settle late. At present it is around 12% but it can be any figure you like. It is a good idea to slip in a very low interest rate in there when buying. It could be that you do settle late — and if the interest rate is low then you are hardly worse off than with a mortgage. If you are selling, push the rate

up as high as possible as a punishment for late settlement. It can be very profitable indeed.

(11) **Finance Box:** If you have to raise finance to purchase (a common practice) then by filling in this box you are making a conditional offer. It will be conditional upon you raising finance as stipulated. No finance = No deal.

The weakness of this condition is that you can reveal to the seller just how precarious your financial position is. If you are paying (say) $500,000 for a property but insert into the box the fact that you need a 90% mortgage ($450,000) you may end up with no deal at all.

The seller may think that you are pushing it up hill and refuse to sell and wait for a stronger buyer with better finances.

Instead of inserting a figure, simply state that the amount required is "sufficient to complete purchase." To drive the point home, do not state which bank you are approaching for the loan. Simply state that the lender is "bank of purchaser's choice." Give yourself at least ten days (that's ten *working* days which is effectively two weeks). Remember it is all negotiable. You can put whatever you like in the box. The seller has the same choices and can accept, reject or amend the offer.

(12) **LIM (Land Information Memorandum)**: Unless supplied, insist on getting one and check it out.

(13) **OIA consents, etc:** These will hardly ever concern investors as they relate to overseas purchasers and very large amounts of cash. If you are in that league you don't need this book.

(14) **Tenancies:** Here you must state either "vacant possession" meaning the property must be empty when you take it, or list the actual tenancies. By listing the tenancies (either commercial or residential) you will be purchasing the property subject to

these tenancies. Ensure that the details are correct. If necessary, use an extra piece paper and staple it into the agreement to be initialled and form part of the agreement.

This is another area fraught with danger. If you state vacant possession, then actually check the property before settling. Many times the seller may give notice to vacate to the tenant who simply ignores it (or can't read more likely).

I recall purchasing a large do-up once with vacant possession, which checked out empty the day before settlement. It was in an incredible mess with shin-deep rubbish in every room. (I kid you not — people do live like that!)

After settlement I went back and to my horror I found half a dozen long-haired layabouts sitting around the open fire place toasting mouldy bread on the end of bent wire coathangers.

My remonstrations went unheeded.

"We're here to stay, man," said one as he rolled over clutching a Green Party pamphlet to his chest.

"Yeah, man," said a skinny doe-eyed woman with two babies at her breast.

"Right on, man," said a third who was so thin the Modern Jazz Quartet could have used his ribs for a xylophone.

It got worse. As I stood there surrounded by rubbish, burnt toast, and babies, a clapped-out car, smoke pouring out from under the bonnet, chugged up to the door and disgorged two more Troglodytes plus more babies.

Maybe the light was attracting them?

I hurriedly had the power cut off.

Blast! It made no difference.

Apparently the place was some sort of hippie hang-out where these types drifted in and out at will. They slept in the rubbish, babies and all. As they paid no rent they simply didn't care.

I would like to report that it took enormous bravery and superb dash on my part to get them to leave. The truth was more down to earth. I gave them each a postdated cheque for $100 provided they left and stayed away permanently. This they understood full well. It still took weeks before they all left but it was worth it.

(15) **Chattels:** This area causes more problems than almost any other part of the agreement. Sellers seem to go haywire after signing on the dotted line and plot and scheme how they can remove everything possible before you move in. If you are the buyer and the chattels are worth something, then list them out in detail — again on a separate piece of paper signed and attached to the agreement. Indeed, it is quite in order to take photos of the chattels and make two sets and have all the parties sign each one.

On several occasions, in my formative years, I bought properties only to find after settlement that the new stove I thought I saw on first inspection had been replaced by a clapped-out rusty wreck. All the good bathroom fittings had disappeared, replaced by cheap plastic ones. Toilet roll holders were unscrewed, together with all the light bulbs, not to mention changed carpets, missing door handles, and naturally, no plants in the garden.

This is the sort of mentality you frequently must deal with.

You better get used to it. It is one of the hazards of the game.

This is why having everything in writing is so important.

7.

Documentation — Part 2 (and some tactics)

In the last chapter we looked at the front page only of a standard Sale and Purchase Agreement. As we discussed, you would be well advised to read all the fine print in the following pages of the agreement because as sure as there are little green apples, one of the pieces of fine print will trip you up some day.

All are vitally important. In particular, note what can happen to you if you fail to settle — whether it be buying or selling. Not only is penalty interest chargeable, but you can be sued for specific performance, made to pay for any losses, or have your deposit forfeited at the very least.

Special conditions

Inside every Agreement for Sale and Purchase is a blank page entitled "Special Conditions" and space at the bottom for signatures.

It is into this space that all your extra terms and conditions are written. Attach a separate piece of paper if there are more conditions than room allows.

It is all very well have a finance condition on the front page (see previous chapter) but there are a host of reasons why you may need other conditions to satisfy your purchase.

Of course, understand one thing: the more conditions you put into an offer the *weaker* the offer looks. Sellers are more impressed with clean unconditional offers. If you make your offer subject to twenty different conditions — all of which have to be satisfied — the seller is merely giving you an option.

Now that's all very well. When dealing with real estate as the buyer you have to remember the words *caveat emptor* — let the buyer beware. When you are the seller this doesn't apply.

Set out below are some of the more common special conditions. *Note carefully that the wording can vary enormously from real estate agent to real estate agent and from lawyer to lawyer. These are only a guide.*

Conditional on Valuer's Report

> "This offer is entirely conditional upon the purchaser obtaining a registered valuation on the herein described property by (day and time). If in the sole opinion of the purchaser the valuation is not satisfactory then the purchaser may cancel this agreement and neither party shall have any claim or right of action against the other. This clause is inserted for the sole benefit of the purchaser."

This a good catch-all clause and together with the finance condition allows you to wriggle out of a deal. Mind you, you must genuinely get a valuation report (how anybody checks I wouldn't know) but even if you don't like the colour of the paper it is typed on this clause should let you off. (At this point I can hear the gnashing of teeth and drumming of manicured fingers on polished desks up and down the country. Know-it-all lawyers will shake clouds of legal dandruff in disagreement. Tough bickies. It is one of the hazards of the game. Smart lawyers can raise an argument on anything including how many angels can dance on the head of a pin. I say it's better to have this type of condition than nothing.)

Conditional on reading and approving leases

> "This agreement is entirely conditional upon the purchaser reading and approving the leases pertaining to the property, such approval to be delivered in writing to the vendor or the vendor's solicitors on or before (date and time). If this approval is not given then this agreement shall become null and void and the purchaser may cancel this agreement (etc, as above)."

This condition would usually be used for commercial property but can be used for residential if there are tenancy agreements (e.g. blocks of flats).

Conditional upon selling another property

> "This offer is entirely conditional upon the purchaser entering into an unconditional sale of his/her/their property at (address) by (date) for a sum of not less than (price). If this sale is not achieved by this date then this agreement shall be null and void (etc etc)"

Now watch it! This clause has to be carefully crafted, otherwise you could end up in trouble. In the example given it says that you must enter into an 'unconditional sale'. At that point, you will be bound to go ahead with the purchase of the property you are trying to buy. Also, an unconditional sale is all very well, but *when* is settlement? Does it coincide with your purchase? Will you need bridging finance? Can you get out of it? Must you sell?

Here's another tip which I have used on more than one occasion when given such an offer. I have actually *bought* the purchaser's property, thereby making their purchase with me unconditional. Then I on-sold their property with hopefully little or no loss. Why not? If the numbers stack up — go for it.

Solicitor's approval

Many years ago a typical solicitor's approval clause would read: "This agreement is entirely conditional upon the approval of the purchaser's solicitor on or before (time and date) etc."

Our solicitor friends started to take umbrage with this as it put the decision to buy or sell onto them which generated much heat and light, as can be imagined. Furthermore, as their atrophied brains focused they argued that this only gave a solicitor the right to approve or disapprove as to the form of the agreement but not the actual agreement itself.

If you must have your solicitor approve of the deal use this mouthful instead:

> "This agreement is expressly subject and conditional upon the purchaser's solicitor's approval as to title, encumbrances, liens, easements and any other regulatory impositions that may relate to the subject property. Such approval to be given in writing by the purchaser's solicitor to the vendor's solicitor by no later than (time and date) after the signing of this agreement."

Now you know why solicitors make so much money.

Time expiry clause

You can have much fun with this one. One of the stressful parts of putting in an offer is waiting for the response. Will the offer be accepted, rejected, or counter-signed? What you must realise is that the moment you put an offer in on a property the agent involved will immediately run around everyone else who has shown an interest and use your offer as a lever to get more offers and start an informal auction going.

That will never do.

So I always put in a simple clause that states:

> "This offer expires at 4 pm (day and date)."

Usually I give 24 hours at the most. This puts pressure on the seller (and the agent, which serves them right). You can always extend the time limit if you want to. The main purpose is to slow the agent down from using your offer as a lever.

There is nothing to stop the seller using the same tactic. I have seen counter-offers come back with time limits putting the pressure back on me instead.

What a cheek!

Note: When you make an offer to purchase, any counter-offer immediately cancels your offer. You can stop right there and not proceed further. Even if one word is changed, your offer is cancelled. Therefore if *you* have an attack of Buyer's Remorse after putting in an offer, you can heave a sigh of relief if the sellers have done anything else but sign the agreement as is.

Bear this in mind. It can be useful to get you out of nasty mistakes.

Miscellaneous

Similar clauses to the above can be used for obtaining:

An engineer's report

Partner's approval

Accountant's approval

Council approval

Change of use

Change of tenancy

Financial reports (e.g. on tenants)

Building inspectors' reports

Bank manager's approval (I wouldn't let them near an agreement but it's up to you)

Psychiatric approval

The list is endless but you get the picture.

The power of delay

Old hands know all the tricks. Delay is the property investor's favourite ploy. Delays buy time and opportunities. Many speculators use all these tricks while they attempt to on-sell or deal the property for a profit without using their own money.

For instance, not paying the deposit is one of them. When purchasing, you may have promised to pay the deposit by a certain date (usually on signing the agreement or when becoming unconditional) but unless it is *demanded in writing* (a Three Day Notice) you can get away with not paying anything until that notice comes. Highly questionable, but frequently done.

Another old trick is finding some minor fault in the LIM report or some petty requisition on the title. You have 15 working days (that's three whole weeks excluding holidays) to accept the title, faults and all. On the 15th day you ask the vendor to correct the faults if any. This can give you many more days, if not weeks, to hold the agreement up while you get the money together, try to on-sell, or rethink the whole exercise.

Yet another delaying tactic is not to settle on the day you are supposed to. If you have thought ahead and kept the penalty interest low on the front page of the agreement then you will be no worse off than if you had borrowed the whole lot on mortgage.

A little sweet-talking and a heap of excuses will buy yet more time without the heavens falling in. Eventually all this will fail and you will be served with a Settlement Notice which gives you 12 working days to cough up or else. (Or a whole month if you are already in possession of the property.)

In the meantime, you are running around trying to find the money or off-load the property for a profit or whatever.

Let me assure you that you will not get away with this sort of tactic too often. It is disgusting, degrading and downright dishonest. No right thinking person would ever contemplate such a thing. Trouble is, that it is used by half the property dealers in town. I would never use such tactics (splutter, cough) and neither should you (hack, splutter, cough).

At this point a disclaimer: If, by any chance, you use the aforementioned tactics and lose your shirt you have no one to blame but yourself.

In reverse, as a seller you should be aware of these tactics and take no prisoners. If there is the slightest default on the part of the buyer, issue the appropriate notice immediately. You don't have to act upon it but at least get it out there.

Auctions

None of these tactics work at auctions. At the fall of the hammer the highest bidder is the owner. If this is you, then no amount of wriggling will get you off the hook. Or will it?

There is one small weakness in this theory. The gap between the fall of the hammer and the signing of the contract can be quite a vulnerable time. In that gap all sorts of nasty things can happen.

I recall a very good friend of mine (not me) using this weakness to advantage. He was desperate to buy a property that was coming up for auction but couldn't get his money together in time. So he cooked up a fiendish plan. Come auction day he and a colleague attended the auction. His colleague was quite unknown to the auctioneer. As the bidding climbed, my friend jerked his hand up and down to ensure that the auctioneer was well aware of his presence. In the meantime his colleague didn't move a muscle. Then at the crucial moment (and this required some exquisite timing) my friend pulled out of the bidding and let his colleague carry on. In a mutual flurry of perspiration and dandruff the property was hammered down — 'Sold' to the unknown bidder hiding behind the pillar!

That was the joke. There was no man behind the pillar. He had disappeared. Confusion reigned. My friend was asked to re-bid. He refused. The auction collapsed.

The delays this caused allowed my friend to gain some valuable days and he finally did buy the property. The vendors were last seen sucking on oxygen masks, the auctioneer drank himself into oblivion, and my friend's colleague went to Surfers for a well-earned holiday.

Don't try this at home folks. It doesn't work every time.

Declarations of Trust

Declarations of Trust are very useful instruments. If you do not want anyone to know that you own a particular property then a Declaration of Trust is the thing for you. What is not realised by many is the fact that it's all public information — anyone can access the name and address of the owner of any property, how much they paid for it, when it was bought and how large the mortgage is. Any cheap computer will get most of the information in a twinkling.

Now this will never do.

As we have seen, money does strange things to people's minds.

Jealousy, greed, and malice make excellent bedfellows.

When purchasing a property, register it into anyone's name you like such as your favourite aunt, son or daughter, or even your bank manager (Joke! Ha ha.) Have your solicitor draw up a Declaration of Trust at the same time which everyone signs, and then file it away.

What the Declaration says in simple English is, that your aunt may own the property on paper, but she is holding it 'in trust' for you. By this means nobody will know your business. You could own 9000 houses and not one of them will appear on the public record in your name.

Mortgages

Mortgages are strange documents and have evolved from two sides of a single sheet of paper 30 years ago, to a bundle thick enough to choke a horse. Mortgages are *not* like hire purchase. A mortgage is money lent to you on the strength of your ownership of a property. You own the property from day one. The mortgagee owns not a single nail or screw of your property. They *do* have the power of sale if you default on the terms — but that is not an easy path.

Once a mortgage was a loan of a fixed amount on which you repaid principal and interest over an agreed term or just paid interest only. These days, a mortgage can be something a little different. Many mortgages today allow for what is termed a 'priority amount'. This is an extra amount over and above what was actually lent to cover the lender in case of default.

It is quite common now for a mortgage of (say) $200,000 to have two years' worth of interest added making the advance, on paper, around the $240,000 level. This allows the lender to let the mortgage drift in case of default, knowing that they can claim up to $240,000 if they let things slide for two years.

This does *not* mean that you can stop paying interest for two years. What it does mean is that the lender can allow special circumstances to arise knowing that they will be covered for all that is owing until you are either forced to sell up or repay what is owing.

'Special circumstances' may be a death or accident by the borrower, fire, family squabbles, mortgagee sales, bun-fights in general, or any event which holds the lender up in enforcing their rights.

It is useful to the borrower as well. It allows the lender to advance more money on mortgage if the need arises, but without refinancing the whole lot all over again.

As already discussed, the world of property investment is paper, paper and still more paper. Some more of the common documents you will come across (and by no means all) are:

> Caveats, leases, variations of lease, assignments of lease, renewal of leases, etc (commercial property); tenancy agreements, bonds, release of bonds (residential); disclosure documents (supposed to tell you all the terms of a mortgage but only serving to confuse matters), settlement notices (see above), property law notices (used when someone is in default in a deal), guarantees (personal or company), shareholders' and directors' resolutions (required

when a company is borrowing money), early release forms (beloved by real estate agents who can get their commission out in double-quick time), general agency or sole agency forms, titles, flats plans, cross lease, freehold, leasehold or unit title, and strata title.

The list is endless. Ask your lawyers to see their forms file. You will be amazed.

8.

Advertising

If you want be successful in real estate then you had better get used to the idea that advertising pays. It is no use relying on real estate agents or signboards alone to lease or sell your property. You must get out there and push, scratch and shove.

The world we live in is saturated with advertising. Every media outlet carries bucketloads of it. TV has wall-to-wall advertising every few minutes. Newspapers are 75% advertising and magazines not much less. The internet is overflowing with adverts and what is stuffed into your letterbox three times a day would keep an open fire burning for a week.

Into this hotch-potch scramble *your* advertising must stand out above the rest — but without the benefit of a Saatchi & Saatchi budget.

As a callow youth I knew nothing about advertising. My first and only salaried job was at age 19 with the Department of Island Territories, then situated on the top floor of the old Auckland Ferry Buildings overlooking the harbour. Already free spirited, I could not believe how the world of petty bureaucrats existed. This short (six month) experience, more than any other, propelled me into property investing by default.

I stared in wonder as the dozen staff signed in every morning in an exercise book placed on the front desk. At 8.30 the chief bureaucrat would silently appear and with a flourish draw a pencil line across the page. If you arrived at 8.31 you signed under the line. Three such latenesses and you were reprimanded in writing.

I immediately caused chaos by standing by the book until 8.35 but not signing. I was not late, I just hadn't signed.

The rest of the day was sheer hell. Cocooned in a room the size of the average suburban bathroom with four older men, all of whom smoked heavily, I tried to add up long lists for bananas, coconuts, lengths of rusty iron piping, and vast quantities of beer. This was done through an ever-thickening haze of smoke accompanied by heavy coughing which showered everything in a pointillism of spittle.

At 10.30am precisely morning tea and sticky buns were served.

At midday everyone stood up as one man and marched out for a one hour lunch.

At 3pm precisely afternoon tea and more sticky buns were served.

At 4.25 there was a loud crash as one dozen pencils hit their respective desks. Everyone sat transfixed looking at the clock.

At 4.30 everyone marched out. The day was over.

It was this mind-numbing existence that got me thinking. Was this all there was to life and work? Seven pounds ten shillings a week and two sticky buns per day?

I played games. I stopped the clock. I forwarded the clock. Chaos reigned. I refused the sticky buns. I left late. I worked through my lunch hour. I was very unpopular. The only diversion was a very beautiful typist in an adjoining room who made eyes at me and passed me suggestive notes.

This was all too much. With my underwear revolving at high speed, I resigned, swearing on oath never to work for a salary again.

And thus it was, dear reader, that I found it necessary to learn all about advertising, for how else does one buy or sell anything?

Don't skimp on advertising

The only true way to get a real estate bargain is to scan the advertisements daily, whether they be newspaper, on the Net, flyers or in agents' windows.

Conversely, the only way to sell real estate is to advertise non-stop. It is useless placing one small advert in a newspaper once a week hoping to get a buyer. The problem with newspapers is that they are current today and fish and chip paper tomorrow. Advertising on the Net lasts longer, but again is limited.

I am constantly staggered at the number of people who refuse to spend money on advertising as it's "too expensive."

When I advertise I do so *every day of the week,* whether it be for sale, for lease, or whatever. Strangely enough, people read the adverts every day and every day brings a fresh crop of interested people who never saw yesterday's advert. Each reply is another chance. Do not skimp on advertising.

Using real estate agents is perfectly acceptable, but again they are being pressured from buyers and sellers, landlords and tenants. With the best will in the world, they cannot be everywhere all the time. Besides, many are incredibly lazy and even if they do get a client they cannot read your mind.

Therefore, wherever possible, I advertise my own stuff. Try it. You will be amazed at the response. If you get no response then your product is no good. The benefit is that you have conducted a mini-market research for a very small cost and can then alter your approach.

An example

I experienced a perfect example of exactly just that. Some friends of mine had their home for sale at $475,000. Despite frequent open homes, banners and advertisements, nothing happened. They were desperate. Six months went by and they were now facing serious problems. They came to me for help and I took it on.

Firstly, I looked at the house. It was a boring 1960s box with the decor of a Hungarian brothel. From appearances, it had nothing to offer. The position was mediocre, to say the least, and the price was set miles too high.

Then I looked at the positive side, and reviewed the advertising that had been conducted previously. All the adverts had emphasised that although it needed TLC it was neat and tidy — which was true. But no one had mentioned that it was a two-storeyed house with two extra bedrooms downstairs as well as three more upstairs.

So with much shouting and yelling, I convinced my friends to let me advertise it for them my way.

Firstly, I didn't mention anything about TLC. Why put people off before they have even come?

Secondly, I lowered the price dramatically by reversing previous adverts. Instead of asking $475,000 I said "best offer over $400,000 buys." That gets the greedies interested and guarantees that the juices start running.

Thirdly, I advertised it as a home and income (which at a stretch it could be) or a work from home property.

Fourthly, I said it was a private sale and the vendors were desperate. (They were.)

Fifthly, I advertised it every day with bold headlines and black borders.

Each advert cost around $110, which sounds a lot, but compare that to a real estate agent's commission of around $20,000.

It would be no exaggeration to say that the phone rang off the hook. I arranged for an open home every afternoon and sure enough, people were coming and going in droves. Not one of them had known that the property had been for sale for over six months.

All of them liked the idea of a home and income or a work from home situation.

Soon offers were flying around, left, right and centre. There were agreements coming out of the top of the house, from under the house, through the middle of the house — from everywhere.

Within seven days it was sold for $450,000 cash unconditional.

I even sold half the furniture for an extra $5000. (Which was a pity, because my friends didn't intend to sell it!) Never mind. It was only good for firewood anyway.

As I wasn't a real estate agent, I could not charge a commission which was a pity. But never mind. My friends fell in love with my wristwatch and bought it for $10,000. By golly, it's tough out there.

In the final analysis, property sells or leases itself. You are more like a doctor at a birth — there to help only if needed. Customers hook themselves on the line you set, and hardly ever get away because they don't want to.

The other lesson from that is that nine times out of ten, if you manage to talk someone into deal under pressure it will fall over later. An unhappy buyer or tenant is as hard to keep as trying to nail custard to the ceiling.

9.

Negotiating the deal

The first thing you must do is tattoo the word Patience on your forehead.

The reason for this is that every seller thinks their property is worth more than it is. Every buyer thinks it's too dear. To get the best deal you have to let the other side down gently, lest you offend them. Offending the seller (or the buyer) is the kiss of death to a deal.

The approach you should take to residential property is entirely different to commercial property and we will deal with each in turn.

Residential

How you negotiate a residential deal depends on whether you are the buyer or the seller.

For buyers the game is played as follows:

(1) When viewing a property never, *never*, run it down to the vendor's face. Residential property is 95 % emotion and running a property down is very bad form indeed.

(2) If the vendor is present when viewing, praise the property to the skies. Go out of your way to speak with the vendor if at all

possible. Tell him (or her) how lovely the property is, how it suits you down to the ground, how much you want to buy it, (even if you feel like throwing up the moment you are out of sight). Heap praise on it. You cannot overdo this tactic and there is a very good reason. Heaping praise and showing enthusiasm puts the idea into the seller's mind that you may be the buyer they have been anxiously awaiting.

(3) In the seller's mind an enthusiastic viewer has already got the chequebook out and that's exactly the idea. If the seller thinks someone is wildly excited, they will naturally expect an offer. It follows that they will be mentally spending the money, planning trips, buying that dream house or running off with the office secretary.

(4) Now, dear reader, this is where you must step back. Keep on praising the property but *do not* make an offer. This will drive the agent and the vendor to distraction. Bitterness will set in, then frustration, then anger and finally despair. Within a few days, a week or two at the most, you will get the message to please, please put in an offer.

(5) Now you have them. They have wound themselves up, mentally spent the money, got the bags packed, the divorce papers ready — and you are going to spoil their party.

How?

Your offer will be very, very low.

Remember: If you don't ask you don't get.

(6) At this point it might be as well to be absent for a while as you will now be the most unpopular person in town. Do not go near the vendor or the agent as there is a real risk that your hair will be parted with the nearest sharp object.

(7) In most cases the vendor will be so bitter and angry it will take a few days before they get over the pain and come back with a counter-offer.

(8) If you have worked the plan correctly, the counter-offer will be quite close to yours as the seller will now be desperate to achieve their dreams.

(9) Raise your offer by only small amounts, one or two thousand at a time. Keep the rises as small as possible.

(10) You will know when the end is nigh. A 'roll' starts, the agent rushes back and forward, the offers and counter-offers get more frequent and the deal will finally be clinched. Have plenty of strong coffee handy as 99% of the time deals are done close to midnight. Congratulations — you have worn the other side down, bought yourself a house. (Not to mention a king-size overdose of caffeine and the shakes.)

When selling:

For sellers, the game plan is just the reverse, with a few extras:

(1) If an enthusiastic buyer turns up, be polite, courteous at all times, and helpful to the extreme, answering all queries.

(2) Be available whenever asked — but under no circumstances show that you are keen to sell.

(3) Feign indifference to whether you sell or not — but without arrogance, even if your palms are sweaty, your bank manager is hammering at the door, and the office secretary has packed and unpacked her bags for the tenth time.

(4) Remember the maxim: *Nothing is more desirable than the unobtainable.* The more you feign indifference, the keener the buyer gets.

(5) This can only be played so far. There comes a point — and you will know it — when the buyer becomes frustrated and will want to rearrange your face unless progress is made.

(6) You can now allow yourself to become keen as well and, with any luck, the pent-up keenness of the buyer will translate into a good offer for you.

(7) If the offer is not good enough, as with the buyer's guide above, drop your price only by small amounts of a few thousand or so at a time.

In both cases (buying and selling) the overall rule is to take your time. There is nothing worse than to sell in haste and to regret at leisure.

Commercial

The rules for negotiation for commercial property are very different to those of residential. Commercial property should be purchased operating on 95% logic and 5% emotion.

The buyer's guide is:

(1) Make no comment one way or the other when viewing the property.

(2) Insist on getting all the paperwork to view (leases, LIM, titles, etc) *before* making an offer. You want to be fully informed prior to, not after the offer is made.

(3) Don't waste anyone's time. You look at the property, you look at the paperwork, you do your sums — and you either walk away or put in an offer.

(4) Negotiations can be glacial at times. As long and hard as it might be, do not mention your financial strengths or weaknesses. Even if you have no idea where the money is coming from, say nothing.

(5) A good deal will always find the money, even if you have to go on bended knees to your favourite aunt.

(6) Use every day the agreement permits to conduct your Due Diligence. If you have ten days, take ten days. If you have 15 days, take them. Make the seller sweat.

(7) Have no qualms about asking for an extension of time so you can consider for a longer period. (Or, more likely, go looking for another favourite aunt to tuck into the deal!)

(8) Only deal with the real estate agent to get more information. Pass no comment on progress and certainly do not ask for an opinion. After all, agents work for the vendor … actually for themselves, as we all know!

(9) Quietly talk to the tenants (if any). You will get more information from them in five minutes than in weeks of other research.

(10) Make one offer and stick to it with only fine tuning. If the gap is too wide, walk away. There are plenty more fish in the sea.

(11) Do not forget about the property if nothing eventuates. File all the records. Half the time, it will be still hanging around months later with the seller now much keener than before. You can then dust it off and have another go.

Selling commercial property:

(1) Make sure the property is tidy and shipshape. This makes negotiations easier all round.

(2) Have all the paperwork ready and make at least ten copies of it all — tedious I know, but unavoidable if you want the negotiations to go easily.

(3) Do not meet the buyer personally, use only the agent. It is not a good look to be seen sweating, shaking and breaking great posterior blasts of wind with anxiety.

(4) Tell your tenants *not to say a word* to any viewers — under pain of death, the rack, thumbscrews, disembowelling and burning at the stake. (See Point 9 above.)

(5) If an offer is made, make one counter-offer (or maybe two at the most). Then look for another buyer because your buyer will be a tyre kicker wasting their time and yours.

(6) If the buyer is an amateur, show no mercy. Amateur commercial property buyers are rare and tend to overpay.

Learn to handle the tension between your desire to do a deal yet remain aloof and in control at the same time. Certainly, do not lose sight of the need to take great care with every deal and each negotiation.

A cautionary tale

I have a friend who was too gung-ho and casual with his negotiations, and at one stage bought everything and anything he could get his hands on. He seemed constantly in the empire building mood — and hang the consequences.

It transpired one day that he was offered a house in a working class suburban street which he was told by the eager and anxious agent was a 'steal'.

He drove himself out to the house (without the agent) and having walked around the property, liked what he saw. Throwing caution to the wind, he tried the back door and found it open. In he went. It was all neat and tidy. He could have taken the lot if he'd been a thief!

Having thoroughly inspected the property, he let himself out, rang up the agent, said it was perfect, made a top offer which was promptly faxed — and just as promptly accepted, and faxed back by return.

Well-pleased with himself, he duly settled for the property a few weeks later, then went back to check it out.

(Note: No negotiations, no care, no fine tuning.)

Strange?!? When he got to the property, a car was in the drive, washing was on the line, the empty beer cartons were still by the side steps, even the large wooden butterfly was still attached to the weatherboards. Somewhere, a dog was barking.

Well, what do you expect from Westies? he thought.

Letting himself through the back door as before, he was aghast to find a gaggle of children playing 'Who can drown the cat?' while a pot boiled over on the stove.

Then Big Momma turned up:

"Who are you?" she yelled. "I don't want any hubcaps today!"

She had obviously mistaken him for the local vicar.

"I have bought your house," my friend insisted — and was promptly thrown out for his pains.

He rang the agent in a rage and demanded an explanation. It was soon forthcoming.

He had bought the wrong house.

The one he had bought, paid for, and now *owned* was across the road.

Horrors!

He hurriedly inspected his new acquisition. Grass grew to the window sills, every window was broken, the paintwork was nonexistent, the roof seemed to have been nailed on by a drunken sailor, and it was only the borer holding hands that stopped the whole property falling down.

It cost thousands to fix — and he only just broke even.

The moral of the story is easy to see.

Had my friend just taken time to negotiate a little, shown some patience, and not been in such a hurry, the disaster would not have occurred.

How, you may ask, do I know all about this person and his terrible deal?

Easy.

That person was me.

10.

Get a good lawyer (and a psychiatrist!)

Get good professionals to assist you, e.g. lawyers, valuers, accountants, bankers, financiers, and (just in case you need one) a psychiatrist.

There is something about many of us in property investment that makes us want to avoid the professions as much as we possibly can. Trying to analyse this isn't easy, but it's probably a control thing. Property investors are do-it-yourselfers, 9-to-5 jobs are out. So are pensions, security, and political correctness.

A few short months in the property world soon knocks the stuffing out of any liberal tendencies. Where once you would give willingly to any just cause, now you must keep your hands firmly in your pockets. The reality of the marketplace makes the investor naturally cautious. If it doesn't, the investor will be taken to the cleaners and end up *receiving* charity instead.

Lawyers

The first professionals you are likely to deal with are the lawyers.

It's a funny thing about some lawyers. There's a sort of 'superiority' thing with many of them. Somehow they are better than all of us. They look down their noses with a hint of disdain and can make you feel totally insignificant.

To make headway in the property investment world, it is vital that you find a good lawyer you can talk to as an equal. One that is available when you phone, can see you at any time, and doesn't mind you calling on the weekend. This is important. A lawyer who will only give you an appointment two or three weeks ahead, and then counts the minutes, stopwatch in hand, to be followed by a bill the size of the national debt, is not for you.

A good property lawyer should preferably come with a sizeable Nominee trust account, or at least keenness to do business with and for you. They should be fully conversant with conveyancing law and procedure (it's surprising how many are not), settle deals one way or the other with the minimum of fuss and expense, be up to scratch with sources of finance in the market, and ensure that leases, agreements, variations, caveats, mortgages etc are all handled promptly and effectively.

They should ensure that you are adequately insured, with a reputable insurance company, that your will is up to date, that your spouse is protected from creditors, and that you set up a Trust or Trusts to protect what assets you can.

All this should be done with speed and efficiency.

By now I expect many of you are rolling on the floor with laughter. The sort of lawyer I have described is the stuff dreams are made of. Time and again I have heard about lawyers being lazy, greedy, slow and uninterested, springing to life only when you don't pay the account within two nanoseconds of it being presented.

Unfortunately, it has to be conceded that a large number are indeed like that. Fortunately, most are not. If you think your lawyer, whom you may have used for years, is not pulling their weight, then there is only one thing to do:

Dump them and get over it.

Hunt around, ask questions and change lawyers. In the property business, one thing is guaranteed for sure. If your lawyer is no good, you won't last six months in the game. I have been blessed with first-rate lawyers over the years, who have saved me from disaster time and again.

Valuers

Another important profession you must deal with are the valuers. Good valuers are hard to find. There are plenty of adequate valuers who will do a so-so job, but a good one is uncommon.

Although rarely exhibiting the superiority of the legal profession, valuers nevertheless come in two grades.

(i) Conservative and (ii) Downright Dangerous.

Conservative valuers are the ones you want every time. It is essential when valuing a property (whether it be for purchase, sale or lease) that you have the best and most accurate figures possible. Once you have these figures, you can do your sums. Remember, it is not obligatory to stick to the figures given. You have free choice one way or the other but at least choose in the knowledge that your decision is based on facts.

Dangerous valuers are those who either are *too* conservative, or (worse still) too optimistic. Completely erroneous numbers will not only lead you astray, but will cost you dear in either lost deals or lost money.

Most valuers will give you a 'kerbside' valuation for a small fee. In other words, an approximate estimate on which you can base your preliminary calculations before obtaining a full-blown written valuation.

In my opinion, valuers give the best deals in town. For a modest fee, (a few hundred dollars will cover most average work) you get a professional document which is accepted by most lenders. If you are borrowing by way of mortgage, or reassessing a rent, a written valuation is a must. It is also very useful when selling (provided it's in your favour) as this kind of proof wipes out any hesitation that buyers may have.

What annoys me, however, is the habit of lenders to advance (say) 75% of valuation or purchase price, whichever is the lower.

This means that if you purchase a property for $250,000 but which values up at $300,000 you will get 75% of $250,000 ($187,500). It should be 75% of $300,000 ($225,000).

The lenders try to bluff by saying that your purchase price is the value notwithstanding an independent valuation. To be consistent, if you paid more than the valuation then you should get 75% of your higher purchase price — but it doesn't work that way.

It gets even sillier. In six or twelve months you can go back to the same lender, provide an updated valuation and get the 75% advance. The purchase price is then irrelevant.

Bankers

This would include all lenders such as trading banks, finance houses, and mortgage brokers.

The trouble with lenders is that they are all frustrated property investors. Put yourself in their position. Day after day they work in an office owned by someone else, sit at a desk owned by someone else and watch millions and millions of dollars go in and out making profits for someone else. It's no wonder that many of those who work for bankers become jealous. They make a fair salary working all year long while noting with green-eyed envy the investor making heaps with little effort (or so they think).

This jealousy manifests itself in several ways, the chief one being a sneering disregard for the worries and needs of the customer. It makes a mockery out of the frequent surveys which ask, "How often does your bank manger contact you to discuss your needs?"

The answer is a fat raspberry every time.

To get the attention of the bankers and money lenders you have to either have borrowed a huge amount or you have to have millions on deposit. This way you impress. The great majority of investors do not fall into this category — and are consequently ignored with a passion.

The lesson from all this is simple: either keep your short-term borrowings (and especially your overdraft) to a minimum for safety reasons, or borrow so much that the lenders have to prop you up.

Accountants

Here's a curious breed if ever there was one. The thought of sitting behind mountains of paper doing sums, adding up columns of figures, and filling in dreary forms would drive most investors to seek refuge in a cloister.

The profession is the complete antithesis of the property investor's world, where imagination, risk-taking, and vision are the tools of the trade.

However, accountants are vital and you'd better get a good one quickly. They should have all the attributes of good lawyers without the huge expense. Again you should have an accountant who is broad minded, will not lose their temper if they can't read your writing, and will fend off the paperwork that the bureaucracy so dearly loves to dump on all and sundry.

Most important, they should produce a reasonable set of accounts within a short time, even if it is 90% wishful thinking.

Psychiatrists

Although I include this profession somewhat tongue-in-cheek, a healthy attitude to investment is a must.

If there is one thing the budding property investor has to do, it is to find the strength to carry on. It is not easy to be self-employed and constantly wondering where the next dollar is coming from.

It requires a special mentality to voluntarily chase after deals that usually go nowhere, handle tenants whose sole ambition is to rip you off, fend off bureaucrats, accountants and lawyers — not to mention put groceries on the table.

Therefore, it is essential that investors seek healthy diversions to offset the dangers of stress. Sport, gardening, hobbies, cooking, house husbandry, stamp collecting — anything to fill in the times when nothing is happening.

If you do not have these diversions, then you will indeed end up on the psychiatrist's couch. (Not that it's anything to be ashamed of; quite the contrary.) But if it can be avoided, so much the better.

I have seen many an investor crippled very early on by the stress of uncertainty, the worry of huge debt, the vagaries of the market and hell of keeping tenants under control.

But take heart. The first five years are the worst. If you can survive these you can survive anything.

11.

Take the time for Due Diligence

The Americans call it Due Diligence, and frankly it's an excellent term.

Due Diligence applies when purchasing a property. It means that you as the purchaser intend to carry out a full inspection of the property, not only physically but all the paperwork as well, before commitment.

When buying either residential or commercial property, Due Diligence is a must. Failing to complete the exercise can result in great misery, if not financial frustration.

It is a reality of life that many people sell their property because there is something wrong with it. This may sound cynical, but it is true enough. Who would willingly sell a property that was excellent in every way?

Of course, there are always genuine reasons for sale such as the three Ds (Death, Divorce and de Bank — see the chapter on Blue Sky). Whatever the reason, the intending purchaser must be very vigilant and hence the Due Diligence time factor must be put to good use and not treated casually.

When purchasing a residential property, whether it be a house, town house, or apartment, many purchasers assume that such relatively simple structures only need a cursory once-over.

Big Mistake!

When putting in a conditional offer, besides the common finance clause, always insist on a Due Diligence clause. Your real estate agent has such pre-written conditions, which in simple English state that you as the purchaser must be satisfied in all respects with matters pertaining to the property. For residential properties, usually 5-10 working days is normal to carry out the checks. (It's as long as several months for commercial.)

Let us deal with residential first:

Houses

A thorough Due Diligence inspection would cover the following:

(1) **Legal description:** Make sure that the land that goes with the house is correctly described. You do not want to find that the land you thought you were buying has been subdivided off and does not belong to your deal. It may not show on the land itself but only in the paperwork. This may sound like a ridiculous error to make but I personally know of many cases where unsuspecting and trusting buyers have signed up for lovely homes on nice pieces of land only to find bulldozers and concrete all over the back yard within a few weeks of moving in. Many people simply do not read or understand agreements. They want to believe what they see and hear.

(2) **Fencing:** Check that the fences are actually on the boundaries. This may require a surveyor. A lot of grief can be avoided if the boundaries are properly established and the fencing matches up. If the fences are falling down or non-existent, it would not

hurt to ask the neighbour, with whom you will share the boundary, what their plans are in terms of fencing. You could be in for a surprise (and extra costs).

(3) **Shared driveways and turning circles** for cars cause much bitterness. If there is a plan for a shared driveway, actually mark out the boundaries to see if you really can turn your car in the area allotted. Most often, good neighbours aren't too worried, but there is always one who will make trouble. Murphy's Law will always be with us, sad to say.

(4) **Swimming pool fences:** This causes much aggravation. If there is a swimming pool on the site, or a large pond, stream, splash pool, spa or anything larger than a birdbath (and the pointy heads are working on them too) then call the City Council to check it out. It may not show in the LIM report. All bodies of water must be fenced by an approved fence, with approved locks. Even doors to patios and decks need to have special locks and notices if a pool is nearby.

I remember one instance I was involved in where I had sold a property, and the purchaser later discovered that the pool fencing was not up to standard. (Not that anyone had told me, of course!) The cunning swine demanded a proper fence with all the trimmings to be erected by me before settlement, or no money on the day.

With the Bank Manager baying at my heels and no spare cash to speak of, a drastic solution had to be found. I discovered that a fence could be made out of anything so long as it was child-proof and complied. Bingo!

I ordered a truckload of second-hand corrugated iron and some old railway sleepers to be delivered to the site. (Cost around $300 as I recall, compared to $4000 for the fancy variety.) I then called round the prospective purchaser and asked him where he would like the corrugated iron and posts to show the new fence and property to best advantage.

His bellows descended on my ears like a tropical cyclone. The upshot was that I gave him an allowance of $800 off the purchase price and he could erect whatever fence he liked. But it was a close thing.

(5) **Drains:** Drains and sewage are boring subjects — that is until you have raw sewage bubbling up all over your garden after the first heavy rain. Again, check with the Council that the sewers are in good repair, that stormwater and sewage are split (i.e. go down different pipes). While you are at it, a plumber should check the internal water pipes and water heating system. If they are on their last legs, make allowances in the price you pay. In fact, check if the property is on a sewage drain at all. Some have septic tanks, which are a whole different story. Note: There's good money for night-soil collectors. $800 per week wages and you get to keep anything you find.

Still on the subject of water, have the plumber check the main waterpipe into the property, that the meter is properly working, and that there are no leaks. It's an expensive business digging up the lawn while trying to track down a leak as the meter spins around at the speed of light.

(6) **Roofing:** The best way to check the roof is to go into the attic and look upwards. If you see constellations of stars looking back, then the roof is full of holes. Now you know the meaning of a five star hotel: Four of them are shining through the roof.

It is not a colossal expense to re-roof in iron but an expense nevertheless. On many occasions I have beaten the price down on a property I was interested in because of the shonky roof. Then after settlement, a sealant gun and some application and lo and behold the stars are gone! Alternatively, pieces of old shirt stuck and painted over the holes does very well indeed and will outlast the roof. To this day, there are innumerable houses in Auckland that have roofs held together with pieces of Pierre Cardin shirts and paint.

Tiles are different. They are either broken or they are not. Make sure there are plenty of spare tiles available for the future.

(7) **Exteriors and guttering:** Brick exteriors usually give little bother. Just check for cracks which could mean the house has settled over time. No big deal, but perhaps for peace of mind an engineer should be called in to ensure the settling has stopped.

Weatherboards are again of little bother. Some will get dry rot but replacing them is no great task (unless the property is three storeys tall). More important is to look along the boards to see if they are straight from one side of the house to the other. If there are major ups and downs and wavy boards, it means that the foundations have shifted. Now that can be serious.

Checking the window frames, either wooden or aluminium, is routine. If they open and shut easily all is well. If they fall out accompanied with a splintering of wood and glass, walk quietly away.

Guttering and downpipes are either good or they are not. Some people go into hysterics when they see a bent downpipe or a piece of rusty guttering. Forget it. It's not that important. However, you could check inside to see if there are water stains around the upper edges of the rooms, meaning that the gutters are overflowing inwards. That means realigning the gutters, a simple job but worth thousands with which to beat the price down.

(8) **LIM Report:** Land Information Memorandum. Each Council will produce a report on the property and it is wise to have one to check out what the Council knows. The cost varies from

around $150 – $400 (a rip-off as we know, but very useful at times). Things to look out for (among the nonsense about "100 year floods", "wind warnings", and "land is unstable" all inserted to cover a Council's backside should the property ever be swamped by a tidal wave and then buried under a million tons of rock blown off a mountain) are permits approved to final stage, pool fencing (see above), historical heritage links or Maori land claims, future road or footpath widenings, rights of way, limitation on number of people on the site (for multi-unit properties) and the like.

Look out especially for granny flats or self-contained rooms that may come with the property. Half the time they are illegal and that will affect your insurance. (Like voiding it, for instance.)

(9) **Foundations:** The earliest houses were built on wooden piles and most have now rotted away. Concrete piles are forever. Wooden piles were used to around the 1920s so anything older than that, check it out. Especially check out wooden piles that have been painted with grey paint to look like concrete. I know many wily property dealers who have used that old trick (ahem).

(10) **Interior:** Moving right along, we now check out the interior, looking for squeaky boards, rotten floors, sagging ceilings, evidence of rats, mice and cockroaches (try the hot water cupboard — they love it there). Wear and tear, upgrading, etc are all obvious. As an extra thrill, drop a marble on the floor to see what happens. If it rolls repeatedly into one corner, either you have an uneven floor, sinking piles or a marble with a bias in it. Also look for cracks in the walls and water stains, especially on the ceilings. The smell of fungus warns of dry rot or long-term wetness somewhere. It all has to be checked out.

Town houses

All the foregoing could equally apply to town houses. The main difference between town houses and regular houses is that they have usually been built in the last 15 – 20 years and are generally more lightweight, using fibre board cladding and plaster to the exterior. Rot can set into the framework easily, so have it checked out carefully. Also remember that making alterations to town houses is difficult without neighbours' consent. Do not assume that you can push out walls, change rooms or add decks, as you can with a regular house on its own land.

Apartments

Again the foregoing applies where common sense dictates. Apartments differ in that they usually have little or no spare land, and can have neighbours up against all four walls. In that case soundproofing is top of the list. Try this experiment:

Take a very large jug of water into the next door apartment or apartments (how you get in is your problem) and standing in the bathroom, pour it gently from the jug into the toilet. (Make sure the lid is up!)

In the meantime, your companion lies on the bed, stands in the kitchen or sits in the lounge in the apartment you are considering purchasing. You will soon learn how good the soundproofing is. Flushing the next door toilet or jumping up and down and yelling at the top of your voice will also tell you a lot about the soundproofing. Make sure you do this experiment with all the apartments that adjoin the one you are interested in.

It is worthwhile putting up with the torrent of abuse, cat scratches, and ill-will generated to avoid not only living in your apartment, but living every moment with the neighbours as well. (And by the way, sound travels both ways. Think about it.)

(See chapters on Commercial & Industrial investment for Due Diligence when buying commercial property.)

12.

Raising finance — Part 1

Basic terms

The big advantage property has over most other forms of investment is that it can be leveraged with little difficulty. *Leveraged* means that with a small amount of money it is possible to 'lever' yourself into a bigger purchase using someone else's money.

At this point many budding investors become confused, so let's clear up some common expressions and common fallacies.

(1) **Freehold, Leasehold:** Owning a property freehold does not mean it is free of mortgages. It means that the land under the building is not leasehold but is held in 'fee simple'. In previous centuries much land was leased to peasant farmers by the Lord of the Land (the Landlord) which caused much aggravation — just as it can today. So a system was developed whereby the farmer could pay a one-off fee and buy the land for ever. It makes my teeth grate when I hear educated people use the term freehold to mean paid off. When you borrow money against the security of the land you are 'encumbering' it. When it is paid off it is 'unencumbered'.

(2) **Mortgage:** Derived from the Latin meaning death grip! As already mentioned, bear in mind carefully that when you have a mortgage on your property it is *not* like hire purchase. If you own a property with a mortgage *you are the owner* and the lender has lent you a mortgage against the security of your ownership. You are the registered proprietor — and don't let anyone tell you otherwise.

(3) **Mortgagor:** One who borrows the money against his/her property.

(4) **Mortgagee:** One who lends the money. Hence Mortgagee Sale (see below).

(5) **Mortgagee Sale:** The lender of money to you secured against your property usually has the right to sell your property if you don't keep to the terms of the mortgage. Now before you lie awake nights worrying that the lender will come knocking if you are a day late with your payment, you can relax. The lender has to go through a lot of hoops before they can sell you up. It's not like hire purchase where the lender legally owns the security until you have paid it off and can turn up with short notice and take it away. Proper notice and time to catch up must be given and then it has to go through the courts and almost always has to go to Public Auction. It can take many months and you have the right to pay off the mortgage or the arrears right up to the fall of the hammer — and thus rescue the situation. Mind you, you may never get another loan off that lender again — but there are plenty of others.

(6) **First, second, third mortgages etc:** These refer to the ranking of mortgages when paying them off. As the name suggests, a first mortgage has the first claim on the equity in a property — hence has the greatest security for the lender. A second mortgage comes in second after the first has been paid in full plus all penalties (if any) and so on, with a third, fourth, or as many as

you like. Second mortgages are common, usually bearing a higher interest rate to reflect the greater risk. Third and subsequent mortgages are rare but not unheard of.

You can get situations where the first mortgage is relatively small and therefore a second mortgage is no big deal. A $300,000 property with a $50,000 first mortgage could easily stand another $100,000 – $150,000 in second or third mortgages if required. Why you would do this is another question, but is found commonly in inter-family loans and Family Trust situations.

(7) **Caveats**: From the Latin 'warning'. Caveats are very powerful instruments which can be registered against the title of the property for a variety of reasons. The main reason is where somebody is claiming an interest in your property. It may be for a legitimate loan to you secured against the property. It is often used in the case of marriage split-ups causing severe heartburn. When a property has been sold pending settlement buyers often protects themselves with a caveat in case the seller goes mad and sells to someone else.

Caveats can cause much grief, and getting rid of unwanted caveats is no easy task. A caveat wrongly registered can lead to massive damages against the caveator if it impedes the legitimate dealing of a property. Therefore if you think it clever to register a caveat on somebody else's property because you happen to dislike them, watch out! They can bite back.

A common way to remove difficult caveats is to lodge a second or third $10 mortgage which must be registered before any caveat. Hence the Registrar has to give a caveator notice that the caveat will be lapsed. Sometimes people have lodged caveats and simply disappeared. Their signature cannot be obtained to release a caveat. In that case, it will lapse and that will be the end of the matter.

Alternatively, if the caveator is wide awake, they must decide whether to let the caveat lapse or fight the registering of a new mortgage. Bitter court cases are fought over these situations and the caveator will have to prove they have a legitimate cause for the caveat to remain. If there is no dispute then partial discharges or caveator's consent forms are readily prepared.

Getting a loan

Despite the plethora of advertisements offering mortgages it is never as easy as it sounds. Lenders are extremely cautious and do not write out the cheque ten minutes after you walk into their office. They say they do, but it's all lies folks! If you read all the flowery words mortgage lenders use to make it sound so easy, you will also always see a rider (in micro-print somewhere) which says something to the effect that normal credit criteria apply.

In simple English this means that the lender is going to go over you with a magnifying glass before they lend you one red cent.

So what to do? The answer is prepare your loan submission very, very carefully. Many people do just that by going to a mortgage broker to prepare the submission for them.

A word on Mortgage Brokers: Many of them are failed ex-bank employees. They couldn't make it in the bank so they become brokers doing the dirty work for the bankers. The bankers like them because the broker sorts out all the tiresome paperwork.

As we all know, most bankers are heartless reptiles. They cannot bear their plush offices and polished desks being contaminated with emotional tears, baby vomit, cigarette ash, or the stench of sweat from a worker's hairy armpits. Far easier to leave all that to patsy mortgage brokers and deal instead in the rarefied atmosphere of big numbers, selling people up, cancelling overdrafts, bouncing cheques and all those other fun things which bankers love to do — especially if it destroys someone's life.

To be fair, I have come across genuine bankers who richly deserve the name in the finest sense. If you are so fortunate to find such a person take out a life insurance policy on them immediately and pray and light candles for them every night without fail. They are a rare and splendid specimen indeed.

Preparing your application

(1) First get ready a **Statement of Position** which shows what you own and what you owe and your net worth. If you own any property show it at today's values, not what you paid for it. Take your time over this. You can puff up the asset side as much as you dare but don't tell lies. A little exaggeration is permitted (how much is your wife's jewellery really worth?) but overstating the truth is only good to a point.

(2) Have **evidence of income** such as your tax returns, salary slip, accountant's statement etc.

(3) Get a **registered valuer's report on the property** beforehand. This way you can control the numbers better. If a valuer's report isn't good enough you can go to another valuer who may give you a better number. It's too late to try this after the application has gone in.

(4) Do an exercise **showing how you will service any loan**. Don't forget to show any rents the property may bring as income. Include your partner's income if they are going into the deal with you. Put every source of income into the equation you possibly can.

(5) **When being interviewed, better to say too little than too much.** Many applicants have blown away their chances by blurting out family secrets that change the picture completely.

(6) Have all the **property's details** with you, e.g. copy of the title, LIM report, structural survey (if it needs one), rental assessments,

pretty colour photos taken from the best angles, anything in fact that makes the deal (and you) look good.

(7) **Shop around.** Be prepared to go to several banks or brokers at once. It is staggering how one bank or broker differs from the other in their reaction to the same deal.

How much to go for?

It pays to ask for a loan that is *bigger* than you actually need. If it is granted then in many cases you can draw down as much as you need and leave the rest for an emergency. (You only pay interest on what you use.)

In most cases getting a loan of less than 70% of a residential property's worth is easy. Banks regard this as a safe margin. If it goes over 75% of the value it gets harder, and at 90% plus it is very hard unless you have a big income, a cast-iron guarantor, or other property as collateral. Generally, banks will lend more on a home you will live in than an investment property. (No, it makes no sense to me either.)

In the case of commercial property loans, the levels are lower again (around 60% on first mortgage and up to 75% on second) which makes absolutely no sense to me at all. But bankers work on the (totally misguided) theory that people will try harder to pay for their homes than their investments.

Types of loans

There are two broad categories:

(a) Interest-only

(b) Principal and interest (fixed or floating interest)

For investors, interest-only is the best option. Principal payments, when added on, can make it almost impossible to service the loan using the income from the property as the only source of revenue. Besides, it takes so long to pay a loan off in this manner, you are better off doing other things with the change.

Of course, it is nice to pay the property off over time, but increasing the value is quicker, cheaper and has the same effect. Whether you decrease the debt or increase your equity through improvements, it all ends up as profit.

There are a huge variety of other types of loans and mortgages all trying to put a different spin on the product. In the end none of them makes much difference. Keep it simple at all times. Fancy mortgages often lead to trouble. The more cogs, wheels, pulleys and rubber bands a mortgage has, the more likely it is to come off the tracks.

100% financing

Just watch an investor's eyes light up when you talk about 100% financing. Yes, it *can* be done and done easily but you must follow the rules: With 100% financing an investor can keep on buying indefinitely with each property adding wealth to the portfolio, income into the bank, status, a flash car, and king-size headaches.

So beware. Do not confuse increasing your portfolio with empire building. Each property must carry itself and wash its face. Empty buildings or those running at huge long-term losses will send you over the financial edge long before you enjoy the fruits of your ego trip.

But wait — what's this?

Heavens! It's the end of the chapter!

Don't worry, dear reader, in the next chapter I will go into 100% financing in detail.

13.

Raising finance — Part 2 *Borrowing the lot!*

Because of the inherent stability of property values, mortgage lenders fall over themselves to lend up to the maximum. History has proven that property values remain static at worst, or, as is more often the case, steadily rise. Occasionally, there are speculative bubble bursts where property values fall, but these are rare and isolated indeed. That is why banks love property, because they will not wake up one morning and find the value has disappeared — as happens with shares, for instance.

To understand how to 100% finance a property deal and still have equity remaining, what you must first realise is that any given property can have several values at the same time. (We discussed some of these when talking about Blue Sky investing.)

These various values are in the main:

(1) Registered valuation (estimate of market value)

(2) Market value

(3) Fire-sale value

(4) Easy terms value

(5) Special appeal value

(6) Government or Council valuation

(7) Insurance or replacement value

By using these differing values, 100% financing (or gearing) is quite possible.

Let's take an example:

You find a nice residential property which can be bought very well. In other words can be bought 'wholesale'. These bargains do not turn up every day. To have a bargain fall into your lap you either have to be incredibly lucky, or work hard at it. Remember, 95% of sellers or buyers do not really have to buy or sell. They might really be bursting to sell or buy but when push comes to shove they do not *have* to in the final analysis.

But, as we discussed earlier, there is a group of people who must sell and they are found in the three Ds of the marketplace, remember:

Death

Divorce

De bank.

These three groups make up 95% of the bargains you will find.

Your job is to find and target them well.

Lesson: If you come under financial pressure sell out early and get it over with while you have the time — hang the pride.

It is from these sources that you will start your 100% financing exercise.

A property that has a market value of (say) $250,000 could be well purchased for $200,000 or less because of one of the three Ds.

Firstly you have to have a use a bit of cunning. Obtain a registered valuer's report on the property confirming the higher figure. (Whatever you do, do *not* tell the valuer what you are paying!)

Next, work out 80% of the valuer's figure to see what you will be able to raise on mortgage. In this exercise \$250,000 x 80% = \$200,000.

Bingo!!

100% finance.

But here comes the tricky bit:

If you go to your salivating banker for an 80% of valuation mortgage he or she will likely grit their teeth and show you the door. (They are jealous, be sure of that.)

Banks like you to put in some 'hurt' money and use the ludicrous excuse that they lend 80% of valuation or purchase price whichever is the lower. They, however, have the money, so what they say goes. You have bought a bargain worth \$250,000 for \$200,000. The bank will only lend 80% of the \$200,000 which is \$160,000, leaving \$40,000 for you to find.

You are being punished for being successful.

Horrors! What to do?

There are several options:

(1) Go to every bank in town and obtain a \$10,000 limit credit card. Four banks x \$10,000 = \$40,000.

(2) Borrow from friends or family by promising a slice of the action (dangerous waters — watch out).

(3) Go to lenders who are sensible and will look at the valuation only.

(4) Borrow more by way of another mortgage against an existing property. (Yours or someone else's — with their permission, of course.)

The quickest way is to go to the fringe lenders (which includes many solicitor's Nominee lending companies) who will look at the valuation only and lend 80% of that. There are many in town, and typically their interest rates are around half as much again as those of a regular trading bank.

But does it matter in the overall scheme of things?

Say you borrow the whole $200,000 from a fringe lender at 12%: Cost per annum = $24,000

Same loan from bank $200,000 x 8.5%: Cost per annum = $17,000

Loss (extra interest cost) in year one = $7000.

This still leaves a paper profit of $43,000 on the purchase.

Now you will go broke if you stay in this situation and here's the queer thing: Six months or so after you made your bargain buy, the purchase price is no longer relevant. No one is interested any more. So wait patiently for at least six months and with gritted teeth go to your friendly bank with an updated valuation (for $250,000 — maybe more) and ask to refinance up to 80% of the new valuation.

Go well-prepared (as described in the last chapter) and with a modicum of luck, you will get your 80% of valuation (viz. $200,000) repaying the existing $160,000 mortgage and the $40,000 change to pay back the numerous threatening credit card companies and estranged friends on the way.

And what do you have now?

A $250,000 property with a $200,000 mortgage at a reasonable interest rate and equity of $50,000.

In other words, your net worth has increased by $50,000 without using a cent of your own.

You are now ready to go out and do it again, and again, and again — increasing your net worth each time. The multiplying effect soon takes over. If you can secure ten such deals and refinance the lot, you will end up with a net worth of $500,000 without a cent of your own invested — plus still own the ten properties, and have a nice income. And you can look the bank manager in the eye instead of grovelling at their feet.

Of course, you can hurry up the process by doing the property up a bit and revaluing it again at a higher figure still (see the chapters on *Doing up houses for fun and profit*). It could well be that your $250,000 property ends up at $300,000 with a make-over. You can then borrow

80% of that (viz. $240,000) putting cash in your pocket, repaying yourself for the work and materials, and perhaps buying yet more property.

How to keep sweet with lenders

If you want to stay in the business, keeping a good name with the lenders is essential. Lenders have long memories. Give them *any* strife and you will never borrow another cent from them again. Fortunately, there are hundreds of mortgage lenders in the market — but not all of them are savoury.

The better ones are the ones you need, as they naturally will have the most flexible terms and the best interest rates. Once you have a good track record with them, all that embarrassing form-filling and truth-stretching is behind you, and mortgages will be almost always granted with a minimum of fuss.

So whatever you do, keep your payments up to date.

If you are short of cash (and which property investor isn't?) then don't pay your bills, borrow from your great aunt, sell something, anything, but *don't miss your mortgage payments.*

It may happen one day that despite your best efforts, you can't make the payment on due date. Bad things do happen, and you must deal with the situation, however unpalatable.

Never let your cheques bounce.

Never let your automatic payments be reversed. Nothing looks worse from a lender's point of view to see 'reversal' or 'dishonour' on their bank statements. If you cannot pay, don't send a dud cheque. If you cannot meet an automatic payment, have it cancelled *beforehand* rather than show a dishonour.

Not all lenders are ogres.

If the problem is short-term, go see them, explain what's happened and ask for an extension of time to make the payment due. You will be pleasantly surprised at the reception you get. Most lenders understand that difficulties can arise from time to time and will be quite happy to wait. If you make a promise to pay some time in the near future *keep that promise*. Your credit will come to no harm in the meantime.

Don't overdo it. Frequent requests for extensions will wear their patience thin. Rare and occasional hiccups are fine. Making a habit of it will not work.

If the lender asks for a penalty for late payment — pay it. It's a small price to be able to go back to the well again.

Secured and unsecured lenders

A secured lender is one that has security for their loan to you, be it a mortgage, caveat, or hire purchase agreement over a chattel (e.g. your car). An unsecured lender gives you, in effect, a personal loan, and has no security (other than your word) — no matter how many bits of paper you have signed.

From my experience, secured lenders are the most relaxed and the most willing to help out if things are difficult. Unsecured lenders are the opposite.

If you are late with a payment they are knocking on the door soon after the payment was due.

How you structure your affairs is your business but a word of advice that bears repeating: Do not use overdrafts from banks to run your business, be they secured or unsecured.

If you must have an overdraft have a very small one of say, less than \$10,000 – \$15,000 and it should go up and down all the time. The problem with overdrafts is that they are always 'on demand'. No matter what you think or believe, the calling up of an overdraft is a constant risk. Many people have got into big problems by having an overdraft secured against their home. On the face of it the overdraft is secured but banks are notorious for calling up 'non-performing' loans.

Especially do not use your home to finance your other business or property investments unless the total borrowings on your home are still modest (say under 75%).

You can and will lose your home if one of your investments goes sour.

Don't do it.

14.

Falling in love can be expensive

One of the most common blunders both home owners and investors commit is overspending on improvements to their properties. Known as over-capitalisation, it simply means that the money spent on improvements is not reflected in any increase in the value of the property being improved.

The typical example is when the home owners decide that a new kitchen is warranted, or build an extension to the house, or even raise the house to provide extra accommodation.

Faulty logic on the part of the owners goes like this: If we spend $50,000 on the house it will not only be a better house but we will increase the value of the house by far more as a bonus.

This faulty reasoning is due to the fact the owners have fallen in love with their property and as a consequence become totally blind to the fact that spending money on improvements often brings little or no financial gain whatsoever. Sometimes just the opposite.

Time and again I have seen people try to argue the price of their property upwards, just because they have built on a wing, or spent a fortune on shifting walls around.

Their reasoning says, We spent the money on the property, therefore it *must* be worth more.

What they do not take into account is the fact that in almost every area of the city there is a limit to what any property may be worth. The price range of a similar home maybe $200,000 – $300,000. No amount of spending will carry it past that upper limit. (See chapter on Blue Sky.)

From this two lessons should be learnt:

(1) If you spend money on a property, get the biggest bang for the bucks. In other words, paint and shiny door handles have more impact than new wiring or new curtains which cost far more. Making the garden pretty and neat will reap greater rewards than laying new carpet. Painting the roof has the same impact as replacing it — at a fraction of the cost. (See chapters on *Doing up houses for fun and profit.*)

(2) If you really feel the urge to spend big, at least do so on a property where there is a greater element of Blue Sky. In some areas, e.g. Auckland's eastern suburbs, it is quite possible to have a house worth $300,000 next door to a house worth a million. In that event, with care it is possible to squeeze the value up — but using extreme caution all the time.

It is also a sad fact that overspending on new properties is a waste of money as well. A great number of new homes and apartments *fall* in value over the first few years of their life, before flattening out and recovering. This applies especially to the cheaper end of the market.

It is so easy to get carried away with improving your home — which in itself is a good thing — but it can be expensive and unrewarding when the time comes to sell.

Improvements should be carried out using this simple formula: ***Every dollar spent should increase the value by three or more dollars. If it doesn't, DON'T DO IT!***

The high costs of buying

When buying or selling a property, it is easy to overlook the extra costs involved. These can be substantial and many deals have been wrecked by not taking these costs into account. Frequently the costs involved are so high that you and your whole family could take a long holiday overseas, all expenses paid, on the same amount.

Therefore, it is imperative that costs are kept as low as possible. These include not only the actual buying and selling costs but the holding costs as well. No stone should be left unturned in your effort to maximise income and minimise outgoings. Frequently, I have seen people make good purchases only to lose all the advantages through sloppy cost control.

The most frequent costs that have to be monitored carefully are:

(1) **Legal costs:** Most people are terrified about going to see a lawyer. As already mentioned, many lawyers give an air of being vastly superior to the rest of us. They are, after all, educated, erudite, skilled in words, and know everything there is to know about the law. Some big city lawyers charge up to $1000 an hour — which is daunting to say the least. Too soon the interview is over. You still had another 100 topics to talk about, but the relentless pressure of the clock and money draining away was all too much. You leave frustrated, confused, and unsure of where matters will go next.

    The bill arrives promptly in the next post.

    This type of lawyer is of no use whatsoever to property investors, and especially beginners. Fortunately, there are a good number of lawyers who are not like that and can be approached more or less as equals. These have to be eagerly sought and, no matter what the embarrassment the change may create, the investor must make that change.

    The most diplomatic way (if you were stuck with the high flying lawyer in the first place) is to explain that you will retain the high flyer for family and personal business, but your investment business must be taken elsewhere.

It's a common fallacy that you can only have one lawyer at a time. That is not the case. You can have as many lawyers as you want, all working on different areas of your life or business.

As far as fees go, a good lawyer charges around $400 – $500 for an average residential property purchase. Any corner dairy lawyer will do for a simple transaction like that. If mortgages need arranging the fees can climb to around $1200. If the lawyers actually find and arrange the mortgages as well then the bill could reach $2000 – $3000 depending on the complexity of the work.

(2) **Mortgage costs:** Besides the lawyer's fees, be aware that frequently there are hefty charges from the lenders. When buying your own home of moderate cost, the lenders all fall over themselves to be as cheap as possible. No fees, or even a contribution towards costs are common. Things change dramatically when you become an investor. Lending institutions have no qualms about lending to investors, but two things immediately stand out:

(a) They will lend less on an investment property

(b) They will frequently charge fees of all kinds over and above the interest charges.

In one such experience, it was necessary for me to refinance $400,000 on a commercial property. To get to the level required I needed a first mortgage of $360,000 and second mortgage of $40,000. The costs associated with this refinance were the highest I have ever paid. For certain reasons I had no option. These costs were:

Broker's fees	$4,500
Lawyer's fees	$2,000
1st Mortgagee 1% fee	$3,600
2nd Mortgage 1% fee	$400
Discharge of old mortgage	$800
Sundries	$500
Other lawyers' fees	$1,500
Total:	**$13,300**

It could have been done more cheaply but things had to be done in a hurry with no time to shop around. The good thing was that I recouped these costs within 6-8 months. The interest on the original first mortgage was 15% (!) while the new mortgages are 6.9% and 11% respectively.

(3) **Accountants:** Many investors try to do their book work in the belief that it is cheaper. Looking after one or two small rentals may be easy enough but it is surprising how quickly the paperwork builds up. Just as with lawyers, it is totally unnecessary to employ a Big City accountant. The small home accountant is just as good. Once your portfolio gets over several millions in value with dozens of tenants then perhaps it may be different.

Having said that, it is frustrating if your accountants produce the annual accounts in manner which is of no use to you. Frequently when raising mortgages or preparing Statements of Position for yourself, their 'prepared' accounts are more damaging than helpful to your cause. It is therefore advisable that you instruct your accountant to prepare your accounts in such a manner as to present the best possible impression to the outsider.

Remember: you are not allowed to tell lies. But neither is it necessary to tell all the truth. Indeed, many investors have two sets of accounts prepared. One which is strictly correct and another set which is for show, as it were. (Some refer to them as "management accounts.")

This form of account-keeping will save you large amounts of money by enabling you to refinance at better rates, or to simply get loans which may have been difficult to organise otherwise.

(4) **Valuers:** Without doubt the best value around. Valuers must be registered to be of any use. Using real estate agents or the like to get sharp and accurate valuations is useless other than as a general guide. When contemplating a purchase, it is imperative to have some idea of the current market value *before* making an offer. As we all want a bargain, doing the homework first is the only way to go. The following are some of the ways to assess a market value before using a registered valuer.

(a) **Look at the CV (Council Valuation) or GV (Government Valuation).**

This is very rough indeed but it's better than nothing. As an extremely rough rule, properties sell anywhere between 10-30% above CV (unless renovations have since been done which makes CVs useless). In other words, if you buy *under* CV, it is almost bound to be a bargain.

(b) **Ask the real estate agent** who is handling the property to give you a printout of the recent sales in the area. Then actually look at these properties and compare them with the one you are considering. Make allowances for state of repair, size of land, etc, but this will help firm up the value for you.

(c) If you have time, **place some small advertisements** in the paper or on the Net for a property that exactly matches the one you are considering and see what sort of response you get. Try different price levels. If the phone rings off the hook or your email overflows then you know you're onto a winner.

(d) **Ring up at least several different registered valuers** who work the area and pretend that you are a complete bunny. Don't ask for a free valuation over the phone but just ask what values are doing in general in the area for the type of property you are looking at. With some luck, you will get some answers that will assist you.

So far it's all been free. Now you must pay:

(e) **Join one of the on-line valuation services** such as "QV on-line", either as a casual or a regular user. With this service you can not only find out the CV, but the size of the property, both land and buildings, its age, what it last sold for and when, the value of surrounding properties, what they sold for and when. All useful stuff. (This and other useful links can be found on my webpage at www.EmpowerEducation.com. Check it out.)

(e) As already mentioned, **ask a valuer to give you a kerbside valuation**, viz. a verbal estimate after a physical inspection. (Not all of them will agree to do this for you.) The fee should be approximately half that of a written valuation. If you don't like what they tell you, take it no further. If you do like it, have it typed up. The average fee for a written valuation is around $200 – $300 for a property under $400,000 (which is a raving bargain!) If you are going to borrow money to assist with the purchase you will have to have a written registered valuer's report in any event.

(f) Before choosing your valuer, ensure that the lender you intend approaching has no problem with that particular valuer. There are some valuers (very few indeed, it must be said) who have blotted their copybook and are not acceptable to the lenders. Over the years a fair number of valuers have been fined or struck off for gross incompetence.

Two extreme examples that I have had experience with will suffice: In one case the valuer valued a property as if it had already been subdivided and made ready as separate plots with houses already built. In fact, it was virtually bare land. He had deliberately written a report with the intent to deceive the lender in the certain knowledge that very few lenders actually go and look at the property in person before approving a loan. Liberal backhanders from a developer had seduced him — and it cost him his career.

In another example I experienced with a commercial property, the valuer had added up all the various rentals to get to a total figure, then made his estimate of the property's value based on that total. The only thing wrong was the rent total included GST, non-recoverable outgoings had not been deducted, and the rents were all jacked up sky-high by the owner in an attempt to push up the value of the whole investment. This caused a mighty ruckus later on when the lender found out that not only were the stated rents actually much lower in total, but they were not market rents in any event.

The valuer was reprimanded severely, and the owner had to sell far more cheaply in order to pay back the lender.

He got off lightly.

Not that valuers are always naughty. Lawyers can be as well. There have been several high-flying cases in recent years where the lawyers have been caught tickling the till and gone to jail. There are still too many lawyers out of circulation at Her Majesty's Pleasure.

As for high-flying so-called Investment Managers, they are no better. Over the years (and even today) there are some glaring examples of these types getting clients into deals that are either straight out crooked or a virtual scam. Either way they lose a lot of their clients' money on the way through.

Now that's one cost you certainly don't need.

Remember the golden rule: ***If it sounds too good to be true, it probably is.***

15.

Don't get too friendly with your tenants

So now you have bought your first investment. Good on you! After the dry horrors of finding, offering and settling the deal, you actually have to live with it and make it pay.

If you think buying a property is nerve-shattering, just wait until you have to deal with prospective tenants. Fully 95% of tenants are good folk who pay their rent, look after the property, and wouldn't put a scratch on the paintwork.

Many investors can go years with no trauma, but it is a hazard of the business that trouble will arise. And when it does it must be faced. Sooner or later, somewhere, somehow the Tenant from Hell will infest one of your properties.

Dealing with that sort of crisis will test your mettle to the limit. It's best that you have the tools and knowledge to handle the problem.

This is where the first rule of dealing with tenants comes in: ***Do not get too friendly.***

It is a common mistake made by many beginners to become friendly. And why not? After all, you have provided an extremely valuable asset (a property) to perfect strangers who are going to pay you a pittance to live in it.

You're naturally nervous. You have a thumping big mortgage eating its head off and every dollar counts. If the rent doesn't roll in your ulcers will be bleeding 24 hours a day.

So by being friendly, your instincts tell you, the tenants will be friendly in return, and will look after your precious investment as if it were their own.

Right?

Wrong!

Being friendly is inevitably taken a sign of weakness by most horror tenants, who will then stab you in the back as quick as look at you.

I made that mistake early on in my career and it almost cost me my sanity.

Having scratched together the money I became the proud owner of a neat three bedroom house in Te Atatu. Advertising it myself (Hah! — who needs agents) I was approached by a stunning young blonde who said that she and her small baby would love to rent it long-term. She was so friendly and grateful that it hurt. What a nice person. A pleasure to have as a tenant.

Being a sucker when it comes to good looking females, I signed her up then and there. This was followed by several phone calls back and forth and ultimately resulted in me helping her actually shift in, moving her furniture around, looking after the baby and generally making a right proper fool of myself. It was when her next rent payment was due that trouble struck. It wasn't paid.

Never mind, thought I. A simple oversight on her part and nothing more. A friendly phone call is all it would need.

How naive can you get?

"Oh I am so sorry," she chirped. "I will bank it this morning without fail, baby has been sick," etc, etc — and I believed it.

It was never banked … and the phone was cut off the next day.

Two rent-starved weeks later and starting to see a glimmer of light, I got into the car determined to face her and sort the matter out, all friendly-like of course. After all, who knows if the sweet young thing wasn't ill herself? Perhaps she was crying out for help, with the baby starving and the bills unpaid. I would gallantly save them both and receive her undying gratitude … and hopefully the rent as well.

It was the car's central locking that saved me that day.

As I pulled into the drive, three of the most ferocious dogs I have ever seen sprang slobbering onto my car, closely followed by a gang of unshaven heavies in singlets, bare feet and huge bellies, who tried to yank open the car door to have a "friendly chat."

As I backed out at top speed, I couldn't help wondering if I was at the wrong address. Where had that huge wooden fence come from? What were all the bottles doing stacked up like mountains? Why were bits of cars lying about? Those white bones in the long grass: were they human or animal?

With a sinking stomach and the frantic tearing up of toilet paper, I realised what my friendliness had cost me. I had let a gang into my precious investment and it was all disintegrating before my eyes.

Had I not been fooled with all the nice words, but been businesslike, doing my homework such as checking references, this would never have happened.

So the lesson to be learnt by all investors is to stay somewhat aloof and distant from your tenants. In this manner you can check their backgrounds, not be taken in by their sweet stories, and when things go wrong deal with the problem without being embarrassed.

Always ensure that a proper tenancy agreement is written up.

As a further step in keeping things correct, always ensure that a proper tenancy agreement is written up, that a full record of the state of the property is prepared before the tenancy commences, that a bond is taken, and that all the references supplied are actually checked out.

Commercial tenants

With commercial tenants it becomes even more important to stay well away. Commercial tenants are generally a better educated class of enemy. Tenancy agreements are replaced by leases which are frequently so complicated they would make a saint swear. Commercial tenants do not hesitate to rush off to their lawyers who will tangle up the simplest problem.

At all times be correct, friendly without being gushy, and never become involved in the personal matters of your tenants — no matter what.

When the rent is being paid and everything is ticking over smoothly it is natural to relax and let your guard down. When you do, it doesn't take long before the first tell-tale signs appear.

Tenants start ringing you up after hours. They start to ask for all sorts of small favours. A light bulb here, a stove element there, a couple of extra days grace to pay the rent and so forth. These are the danger signals.

This sort of petty whining can be forestalled by writing into your rental agreements or leases that minor repairs are the tenant's responsibility. This simple act will remove 90% of complaints and let you sleep better at nights.

Use a PO Box

One last warning: Never, never give any of your tenants your home address. Indeed, you should remove your address from the phone book. It is a simple precaution but you can never tell.

Put yourself in your tenant's shoes. The rent is in arrears, the partner has run off with the postie, you've just been made redundant and all your home brew has gone sour. The first reaction is to kick big holes in the walls (your walls remember!) and then go to the landlord to get the rent deferred. If they have your address you run the real risk of having a very upset and angry tenant appearing at your front door late at night demanding that you bail them out or they'll punch your lights out.

Giving a PO Box number as your address is a very effective precaution — or better still, the address of some real estate agent or bank manager you particularly dislike.

In summary, even if your better nature says otherwise, have the minimum personal contact with your tenants, communicate in writing or through a property manager. Indeed, if possible, do everything through a third party. In this way you may just survive the first critical years of property ownership.

Postscript: No doubt, dear reader, you are wondering how I got rid of the gang which took over my house. Ah … that's another story. Suffice to say that it takes one gang to get rid of another. More another day.

16.

Be ever vigilant

There are some strange people about.

One of the hazards of the property game is that it attracts some weird people. This is due to the large monetary numbers that get bandied about — plus a misguided sense of power.

Many people think that just because you are the landlord of a couple of moth-eaten flats it automatically makes you a millionaire.

It is true that since time began the very rich have made the bulk of their fortunes out of property. It is equally true that huge *losses* have been made in the same field — something that is frequently overlooked by the envious.

Most investors know that there are some known risks in property investment which do not need long explanations. These include absconding tenants, damaged property, unpaid power bills and the like.

What is not generally appreciated is that the whole business is riddled with con-artists who are prepared to lie, cheat and commit criminal acts just to make a dishonest buck.

Unfortunately in their outrageous efforts to get rich quick they can take down the honest and innocent investor on the way.

Here are some true stories I was personally involved with over the years. These will give you some idea of the breathtaking cheek of some people who tried high-tech swindles — and sometimes got away with them.

The year is 1989. New Zealand is mired in deep depression after the stockmarket crash of 1987. Buildings lie about every where, some half-finished, some empty, many with declining values and desperate owners.

The housing market is flat. Interest rates are still at 18%.

I was marooned in my office, bored, wondering where it all was heading when I got a phone call from two breathless women real estate agents.

Would I like to meet a property buyer from the States who had already bought $40 million dollars worth of real estate and wanted more? Would I be interested in selling something?

Would I what!

With some haste and anticipation, an appointment was made for 10 the next morning at my office. It was going to be an interesting day.

Next morning at 10 sharp a magnificent Mercedes Benz car drew up and out stepped the American buyer accompanied by a young boy no older than 12 or 13 who was introduced as his son, together with the two agents who twittered about like demented butterflies.

I was introduced to 'Mike' and took an instant dislike to him.

He was very short and very fat. His pot belly fell over his belt in a bouncing wave. His shirt was open all the way down with festoons of gold chains hanging around his oily sun-tanned neck. On each finger, diamond and gold rings outshone each other.

His phoney American accent completed the picture. What and who was this fellow, I wondered. And who was the young boy?

Then he started big-noting. What he hadn't already bought wasn't worth buying. He had unconditionally purchased one tower block after another to the value of $100 million (up from yesterday, note). He had bought a well-known restaurant chain for $20 million, a mansion for $5 million, and he would buy at least another $100 million dollars worth before he was finished.

All the while the two real estate agents sat with eyes wide and shiny with wonder.

My eyes were shiny as well but more from tears of suppressed laughter. He agreed to buy one of my properties sight unseen, then and there, and would offer $5 million cash unconditional for it.

The two agents scribbled and scribbled while he talked on and on. I began falling off my chair with boredom.

All was signed with a flourish but before I signed as well, I had one very small teensy-weensy question:

Could he please put down the 10% deposit of $500,000?

His reaction was interesting. No, he never paid deposits. That was beneath him. His lawyers handled all that.

I agreed. It was also beneath me to sign unconditional contracts without a deposit. My lawyers would look after that matter as well.

On that high note he swept out with his entourage, leaving me with only an Auckland phone number should he be required.

That was a big mistake on his part.

The limousine had not disappeared from sight before I was ringing the number he gave. It turned out to be a flea-pit motel in deepest darkest Auckland.

I phoned the car dealer who had supplied the car. No, he hadn't been paid either, but he had been promised payment and had sent in the invoice.

I phoned the manager of the real estate firm involved. With a trembling voice he confirmed that they had spent over $2000 wining and dining our friend and his son for the past two weeks.

My last call was to the police. It later turned out that he was a well known con-man from Wellington (where else?) and his 'son' was his toy-boy.

He got three years.

The agents got sacked.

The car dealer and the motel lost thousands.

On the bright side, a large number of lawyers were delirious with joy as they contemplated the fees they would charge for untangling the mess. It would take years.

If you thought that story was strange, how about this one:

For my sins, and in a bout of delirium, I purchased a large block of twelve rundown flats for $400,000 in South Auckland. (What made me do it I do not know.)

Collecting rents from the Troglodytes that infested the block was not a job for the faint-hearted.

I started well enough. I visited every tenant, gave each a note stating how much the rent was and a pay-in slip. Each was told to pay his or her rent into a designated bank, either directly or by way of automatic payment.

On rent day only three rents made it into the account and all were short. Furious, I drove to the flats (no one had phones, or if they did they were cut off) and hammered on a dozen doors. Three sleepy tenants answered. Two paid up.

Excellent. I now had five rents out of twelve. Then I went about banging on more doors. It resulted in nothing. In the afternoon I drove down again. (This was getting expensive.)

One more tenant — but he couldn't pay.

Next morning was Sunday. Surely first thing Sunday morning would be the time to get them.

Arriving at 8 am, I pounded on the doors again. Only one answered and paid — but he was short by $20. Two others promised to pay if I called back on Monday. The rest were asleep in a haze of alcohol and steaming boiled fish heads.

This was all too much.

Back I charged on Sunday afternoon. Amid a splintering of doors, kicking of dogs, a tide of fleas making an instant home on my legs, and despite my best efforts, I collected nothing more that day.

This really was too much. I had obviously made a mistake.

I did try to get a real estate agent to manage them but he resigned after six rent-starved weeks.

Using lateral thinking, I advertised them for sale for $500,000, on easy terms. As luck would have it, an out-of-towner bought the block on $20,000 deposit and the balance in two years at 9% interest payable quarterly. A small paper profit for me and no worries.

I never saw the interest. Not one cent was paid.

This out-of-towner wasn't as silly as he looked. He was pocketing the rent and never intended to pay the interest. A nice little earner if you manage it. He had figured that if he could hang on for six months or more he would double his deposit.

Issuing a Property Law Notice isn't that simple. There are certain time procedures required. It could be well over six months before I could get the property back, while the buyer made off with the takings.

It was a tense time. Where before I was suffering from acute rent starvation now it was acute interest starvation. I had bills to pay too!

Eventually I repossessed the block but that was only the beginning of the story.

Would you believe it? The two sons of the previous buyer turned up. Could they buy the flats on similar terms? They would give me a nice Japanese car and $10,000 in cash as the down payment. Same terms as before.

There was obviously something in the water in their part of the country or maybe the moon was full. Anyway, this was ridiculous but what was there to lose? I took the deal.

The car and their cash came to $20,000 so I was ahead for the first time.

Dear reader, if you think that was the end of the story, I am sorry to tell you that it was still only the beginning.

The two sons defaulted (what else?) and once again I took the property back, and re-advertised it for sale.

I swear the rest is true. Another buyer from the same city as the first two appeared. (There definitely is something in the water.) This time he had $50,000 cash down payment. I took the deal.

Wait for it. About three months later, he phoned up very upset up and in tears. His business had folded. Would I let him off the deal if I could keep the deposit?

Well, what could I do with the poor fellow? Of course I let him off and kept his deposit. It was the only honourable course of action (ahem).

I had now sold the same block *three* times and was doing very nicely. One could make a nice living reselling the same property over and again. The party could go on for years.

Truth is stranger than fiction, as the saying goes. For the fourth time I advertised the block. This time a farmer took the bait. He would pay his deposit by way of $10,000 cash, a bulldozer, a caravan, a monster truck, and a four-wheel drive jeep. Total value of the trades: $100,000.

I knew nothing about this type of machinery, but I took the deal.

One week later, I was reduced to a gibbering wreck. All the vehicles had had their ownership papers altered to make them appear ten years younger. The actual estimated value was around $50,000.

The buyer naturally denied he had altered the papers.

There were months of pushing and shoving, threats and counter-threats. The vehicles stayed in storage, my bank manager was trying to beat down my door and I was starving to death.

Eventually the buyer agreed to pay (without prejudice) a further $25,000 in full and final settlement. I was free to sell the vehicles.

They raised $100,000!

These were but a few of the real life stories that actually happened to me. (Names and addresses are available upon payment of a substantial fee.)

At times it really is terribly hard to make money out of real estate.

17.

Selling on low deposit: rent-to-buy or 'Wrap' deals

It follows from the previous chapters that obtaining finance is never as easy as it sounds or looks. Don't we all wish that the person who writes the advertisements for the lenders was also the one who approves the loans? So why not take advantage of the fact the lenders are never as generous as their publicity suggests?

It is only in recent times that banks have extended their lending to 80%, 90% or even 95% of a property's value. In the dark old days, (i.e. pre-1980s) house mortgages were almost impossible to obtain. It's hard to believe now, but most people had to rent and save a very large deposit at the same time.

The only lenders were building societies, insurance companies and the Government through the then Housing Corporation. Even in these cases, you had to wait up to five years to win the right to obtain a mortgage by way of ballot — and then perhaps only 60% of a property's value. Looking back, we must have all been crazy. There were even 'ballot-winning parties' when someone got lucky.

From this madhouse mortgage system, solicitors' Nominee mortgage companies sprang up, allowing Mums and Dads (and property dealers) to buy whenever they were ready.

Better still, nominee companies had little trouble in permitting dealers to on-sell under long-term agreements. This was not possible from traditional lenders as all their mortgages contained clauses which said in effect any disposition (sale) of the property allowed them to immediately call up the mortgage.

Today, as then, there are many tens of thousands of good, honest, hard-working people who are forced into renting because they do not qualify for a mortgage. The problem could be an income that's too small, some previous bad credit history, being self-employed, or a solo mum with part-time work where income is very uncertain. You can be sure that banks will never lend to someone if there has been some bother in the past.

To my mind, if someone can afford to pay rent — why not a mortgage?

If you provide the finance to buy a house for someone who has fallen into the cracks, not only are you doing a social service, but you richly deserve a medal as well. (Making a thundering great profit on the way is merely an accident.)

The other main use of selling on low deposit is that you widen the field of buyers by at least 50% or more. People who never thought they could ever own a property (residential or commercial) are suddenly in the hunt.

Types of low deposit sales

There are myriad schemes for selling on low deposit, many of them questionable to say the least. Some are complete rip-offs and have featured in the news media in recent times, especially where good folk have lost their homes in the process. Stay away from anything that is patently dodgy.

There is plenty of profit in regular deals.

The term 'Wrap' (short for wraparound mortgage) is another Americanism but the system has been used by property dealers for decades in New Zealand — to my certain knowledge for at least 50 years, possibly more.

The basic principle is to provide a mechanism that allows purchasers with limited funds to purchase a property with a very small, or even nil, deposit.

Some of the more popular schemes go by various names such as:

(1) Long-term agreement for sale and purchase

(2) Sale by agreement

(3) Rent to buy

(4) Wrap mortgage

(5) Lease with compulsory purchase

(6) Lease with option to purchase

(7) Long-term settlement with prior access.

The general rule is that by one means or another, you the seller can divest yourself of a property to someone else (who in truth can probably barely afford it). It is a very useful tool to get rid of some 'sticky' or pain-in-the-backside investment that you couldn't sell otherwise. You may also get a price that you may never get selling any other way.

All the above schemes, no matter how they are dressed up, essentially provide the same service: **a small amount down and the rest on easy terms.**

Sound familiar?

Yes, it is the same principle as Hire Purchase on motor vehicles and washing machines. Legally, it is quite different but, in effect, it is the same. The ownership stays with you while someone else pays.

When the final amount due is paid, ownership passes to them.

The essential point is that under any one of these schemes *you* remain the owner (viz. registered proprietor) and can raise mortgages etc as before, whether you have sold by way of agreement or not. When you do sell under these arrangements, while you remain the owner you also become the 'unpaid vendor'. The buyer has agreed to buy the property now but with full settlement at some agreed date in the future.

Be aware that under all these schemes the buyer can (and should) lodge a caveat on the title to protect their interest. In anticipation of this you must include in the terms of sale a condition which states that the buyer will lift the caveat temporarily any time you need to roll over a mortgage, or refinance. Failure to do this can lead to very sticky situations.

Let me tell you of some other advantages and disadvantages that may not be that obvious at first glance.

Advantages

(1) You get a better price more easily (see above).

(2) The buyer will pay all the rates, insurance, and upkeep — which saves you a great deal of bother.

(3) The deposit can be any figure you like. My advice is to get as much as you can. A very small deposit only encourages buyers to walk away if it gets too hard.

(4) The deposit is, in effect, a type of bond. If the buyer defaults, you get to keep the deposit as liquidated damages.

(5) The interest the buyer pays will (or should) cover your interest payments. Correctly set up, you are effectively baby-sitting the property until cash-up time.

(6) Both residential and commercial property lend themselves to these types of deal.

(7) If the buyer defaults, taking back the property is much easier than a mortgagee sale.

(8) There could be some positive GST implications — which your accountant or lawyer will explain to you.

Disadvantages

(1) When you sell, you have *locked in* the agreed price. Any future growth in property values will not be obtainable.

(2) You have to wait years sometimes (depending on the deal) before you see your money and profit back.

(3) Buyers often strike problems — making payment or refinancing to pay you out. This is a hazard of the game. After all, you are usually selling to people who have been turned down by regular lenders. My advice: don't be too tough at first. Bend over backwards to assist. You may end up all over the news media as that 'heartless' property speculator who threw low-income Mum, Dad and the kids into the street. That is not good for business.

(4) If you do deals like this regularly you will be classed as a dealer with all the implications that brings. Again, seek advice from your accountant or lawyer on how to set up these deals and what legal structures to use before rushing in.

(5) These deals work best at the cheap end of the residential market. This means that margins will be tight. However, there is no reason you cannot do these deals with million dollar properties, just that your buyers are usually very sophisticated and making a profit is that much harder to achieve.

Having just given you advice on not being too hard on buyers under these schemes, let me tell you that if a buyer gives you a hard time then throw the book at them. (In fact, handled correctly, it can be very profitable, as we have seen.)

Where to start

First, catch your cheap property. Although a Wrap deal can be done with any property (and at any price), it is prudent to start with a property that you have purchased well under valuation. The sound reason for this is that when you on-sell there has to be a fair chance that the new owner can refinance out of the deal at some time and give you a profit. If it is overpriced then trouble will surely strike.

On the other hand, there are many dealers who don't care about over-pricing. They take the view that property prices will surely rise so they may as well get in first. Alternatively, they *hope* the new buyer will default because the terms are too tough, they then get the property back and start again.

Most buyers with low deposits where the bank has said No are too naive to know values, and are so grateful they will buy anything and take no notice of the price asked for a chance to buy.

You can take your pick. I prefer the first method of buying cheap and selling at market price. On the other hand, if a property does come back through the buyer's default, it's party-time! You get to keep the deposit, get the house back, and then sell it again for another deposit.

Having bought cheaply, at say 80% of valuation, you finance it wherever you can. With any luck, you get 80% of valuation which means you have no money invested. Then you sell it at full market price under the Wrap scheme.

An example

(1) Purchase a property at $200,000 which is valued at $250,000. One way or the other, you have made a profit of $50,000 at least on paper. Your mortgages are $200,000. (So far so good.)

(2) Sell the same property for $250,000 on $10,000 deposit.

You now have $10,000 in the hand you didn't have before and still $40,000 profit to go.

(3) Take the balance due, ($240,000), under a Wrap or Sale by Agreement deal.

Practical steps

A Wrap or Sale by Agreement is actually a private loan agreement between yourself and the buyer. As the word Wrap suggests it wraps around your own mortgages and ownership of the property.

Your funding and ownership stay exactly the same. You remain the actual owner and you remain liable for the mortgage(s) you raised on the property in the first place.

The buyer enters into a written agreement with you which essentially is a type of hire-purchase agreement (legal purists will shudder at this definition, but too bad).

The buyer gets the use of the property on certain terms but you remain the owner until the last payment is made.

As we discussed, that means that if they default you can hook the property back and drive away with it (as it were). It's much quicker and simpler then a mortgagee sale.

The buyer makes certain agreed principal and interest payments during the term of the loan from which you, in turn, apply to pay your mortgage. Some residential Wrappers collect a single all-inclusive weekly or fortnightly payment which covers mortgage payments, rates, insurance, even water to help the purchaser's budget (and reduce the Wrapper's risk: Any default of these payments can mean calling up the loan as well.)

How long should the deal be?

It depends on your time-frame. I find that two or three years at the most is best. You get to see your profit sooner, and it follows that there are fewer problems if the time is shorter. The purchaser is well aware that they must refinance with a regular bank within that time — so the pressure is on.

Oddly enough, the banks don't seem to have that much trouble refinancing people who are already in their own home, even if it was bought under a wrap scheme. It's all politics, of course. Banks do not want to be seen as being instrumental in throwing people out of their own homes by being too hard.

As long as you, the dealer, can give a hand-on-heart statement to the bank saying (ahem) that the buyers were angels the whole time you had them and (ahem) never missed a beat, all will be sweet, and the refinance will go through.

There are some dealers who arrange 25 year loans on their properties then wrap a similar length, or longer, loan to the buyer. I cannot see the point. I want the profit out sooner rather than later. But, to each their own.

To keep the time factor short, I have often used the discount method to assist with the hurry-along. If a property is sold for (say) $50,000 profit, I will write into the agreement that if the buyer refinances out and repays the lot within 12 months time then there is a $10,000 discount. Believe me, they work their little backsides off to get the discount. Great!

Money early is worth more than money later.

The purchaser's rights

The purchaser does have the absolute right to use the property as their own in all respects under any such type of agreement. You cannot go around and threaten them on some pretext unless it is strictly to do with the new owner's obligations under the agreement.

You cannot alter the agreed repayments, the price or terms unless by mutual consent. You cannot sell to another, complain about the colour schemes, object to the race or types that may live there, (however, your agreement may make the deal subject to occupation by the purchaser's family) even if it does give you the dry horrors and shakes when you see what they doing to the property. The only limit is if they start destroying it.

All these can only come into effect upon the default of the purchaser under the agreement. Then again, you must issue a Default Notice or Property Law Notice which gives them up to a month to rectify matters.

This all has to be done legally or it will be *you* paying the penalty instead.

As already mentioned, further protection for the purchaser comes with their right to register a caveat on the title of the property to protect their interest. A caveat bars any further dealings with the property. While it sits there on the title a caveat can be very frustrating. Remember, it is wise to insert into the original agreement for Sale and Purchase that you, as vendor can register fresh or changed mortgages during the life of the agreement and the new owner must agree.

This will allow you to refinance and register variations of the mortgage without trouble during the life of the deal. It's good practice to ensure that you can refinance *only up to the level of the debt owed to you by the purchaser*. This allows you to pull a few thousand out of the deal in advance now and then before final settlement.

Lease with compulsory/option to buy

Another wrinkle in the low deposit selling game is to sell property under a *lease with an option to buy* or a *lease with a compulsory buy*. Both can be very useful tools indeed.

Option to buy

This is different from the Wrap deals in that the purchaser is not compelled to purchase the property. But in many respects it ends up the same — with some great advantages.

The document used is similar to any tenancy or commercial lease (depending whether it is a residential or commercial property). The tenant is obliged, as under any regular tenancy lease agreement, to pay a certain amount per week or per month. A fixed period is given, and I always insist that rates, water charges, and insurance are paid, and that all maintenance etc is carried out/paid for by the tenant. The twist comes in the last special paragraph where the tenant is given the right to purchase the property by a certain date at a certain price.

Furthermore, I always ask for a substantial deposit in "anticipation of the tenants exercising their right to purchase." Something like $10,000 or $20,000 will do, but any figure acceptable to both parties is fine, thank you. This deposit acts as a giant bond in the event the tenant shoots through or messes the place up.

It is, of course, totally refundable (and must state so in the agreement) but note the lease wording should include something to the effect that the refund is repayable but "less any costs, damages etc properly payable by the tenant under the terms of this agreement." It's a big insurance policy in effect — and very comforting too.

You can see the conundrum the tenant is now in. They have paid all the outgoings and maintenance and probably improved the property as well. They are almost compelled to buy — but of course they do have the absolute right to walk away if they choose.

Just to twist the tail of the whole deal again, I frequently insert an extra clause. This states that in the event the tenant *does* exercise their option to purchase then (say) 25% of all rent paid will be treated as paid towards the purchase price. If they do *not* purchase they get nothing back. Just think of the pressure on the tenant-cum-purchaser. A sale is virtually in the bag.

Of course, the genuine option plan makes the whole thing non-taxable as it is a real option after all. Only when the tenant does exercise the option does tax, if any, come into the picture. The advantages are obvious. See your accountant first!

Lease with compulsory purchase

This is exactly the same as an option except the tenant *must* buy the property at the agreed price within the agreed term. This sort of deal is used where the tenant/purchaser has little or no deposit but may have decent earnings. All the clauses mentioned above (especially the deposit) would apply but in this case they have to buy. But if they don't buy, do you really care?

18.

Commercial & industrial — Part 1

The investment into commercial or industrial property requires a complete change of mindset.

Residential investment is run on emotion. Commercial is run on logic.

If you wish to be a commercial investor it is imperative that logic runs your decisions. A building should not be purchased because it looks pretty or has nicely coloured walls. A commercial building must be dissected with surgical precision prior to purchase. Emotion must not be involved.

General

Matters that must be broadly checked when considering a commercial purchase include:

(1) **Position** — you can always change the property, but you cannot change its position. Is it easy to get access? (Think from a tenant's point of view — not yours). Is it close to motorways, rail, airport,

population centres? Can workers get there easily? Can management, for that matter? How good is the parking?

(2) **Future potential** — What are the prospects for the area? Is it declining, rising, or going sideways? Are any future developments projected that will affect the area for good or bad?

(3) **Tenants** — What is the calibre of the tenant or tenants? Have they substance? Does it matter?

(4) **Lease(s)** — Check the leases carefully and understand them.

(5) **Condition** — What is the state of repair? Who is liable for repairs? What about pollution?

(6) **Return on investment** — Is the return (i.e. yield) good, bad or indifferent? High returns are not necessarily good.

(7) **Versatility** — Would the property appeal to a multitude of tenants or is it purpose-built with special features?

(8) **Status** — Would you be proud to own it? (OK, that's emotion — I changed my mind.)

The list goes on and varies from one type of property to another, so let's be more specific.

Types of property and dealing with leases

Commercial property falls into three broad categories:

Retail: Shops or any building where passing trade or the general public are invited.

Office: Commonly found with retail or alone, and often above the retail areas on the ground floor.

Industrial: Places where things are manufactured or services provided — but not necessarily where the general public are walking by.

The first thing to realise is that with all three broad categories, there are no firm boundaries, but a lot of fuzzy edges. Often retail and industrial plus offices are mixed together in one property. Shops have factories behind them. Factories have shops in front. Both may have offices — or maybe not.

The only method that can be used to get to grips with what you are looking at is to ask:

"What is the predominant use of the property?"

The rest are ancillary to the main purpose.

Once the main purpose of the building is ascertained, the calculations begin. Any retail area must be viewed as its stands together with any office, and any factory areas evaluated separately. The rentals for each are different, even within the same building.

Generally, retail commands the highest price, followed by office, followed by factory or storage areas. This is not always so and you must take care to get the numbers right.

At this point the services of a registered valuer are important. If you are not certain, get the property reassessed for its various rentals.

Of course, the rentals currently being paid will be of assistance, but the joke is that often as not the vendor (or landlord) has never worked out the different rents, and is charging a global figure for the whole building.

For example, we may have a property which is one third retail, one third office, and one third factory. A global rental of (say) $50,000 p.a. is being paid. If the building is 500 m^2 in area (approx. 5500 sq. ft.) we have a average rental of $5.50 per sq. ft.

(Note that rental areas are still commonly quoted in square feet (psf) while land is almost always in square metres (m^2). We will use square feet from here on.)

However, on analysis, a different picture could emerge — and this is where the juices start running. It staggers me how often this scenario turns up providing rich pickings for the investor.

Taking our above example, and using likely figures the rent should be:

Retail one third 1833 sq ft @ $20 psf	$36,666 p.a.
Office one third 1833 sq ft @ $15 psf	$27,495 p.a.
Factory one third 1833 sq ft @ $6 psf	$10,998 p.a.
Total	**$75,159 p.a.**

This is but a model but it makes the point. There could be 50% more rent in your pocket than at present. Better than a poke in the eye with a burnt stick.

Now this is all very well and good, but if there is a lease in place you cannot bowl in and increase the rent just because your figures say so. Therefore the next step is to see when the rent is next up for review. Great patience is required at this point, for the truth is that while the lease is in place the landlord is powerless to change anything so long as the tenant is behaving.

A landlord only gets a few shots in any one period to use their powers under a lease. It's your job to create as many opportunities to break the lease to your advantage. Be careful — you don't want to lose the tenant. Overplaying your hand can be financially fatal. All you want is to get your feet under the table with the tenant and sort matters out — to your advantage of course.

The common ways to break a lease early are:

(1) Find a fault that the tenant is committing, even if minor. Compare the lease conditions line by line with the reality and see if you can make something out of this fault.

(2) When a tenant asks for a favour that requires some effort on your part, make it a condition that the lease is reviewed.

(3) If the lease is up for review anyway, bear in mind that the tenant may be locked into the lease and must accept a new rental if backed by valuers' reports. Huge fights can break out when this happens and it's all jolly good fun … but you must win in the end within reason.

Warning: All the above points will turn to custard if the tenant walks out. It requires a delicate but firm hand and enough brains to back down if things are not going well. There will be another day — be sure of it.

Types of lease

A lease can be a most complicated document, open to all sorts of interpretations, and can come in a bewildering variety of forms.

Typical:

(a) **Exchange of letters** — suitable for casual letting and small areas.

(b) Basic commercial ***Agreement to Lease*** which is only a few pages long but sets the terms out. (Often as not, this is as far as the lease gets.)

(c) A **full formal lease** which can be up to 50 pages long repeating everything in an Agreement to Lease plus every other contingency that can ever be imagined.

The Auckland District Law Society puts out a good version, as do commercial leasing agents, while many solicitors prefer their own. (More fees of course!)

Ninety percent of the waffle in a commercial lease is never read, being standard stuff, but some areas are very important.

When reading any type of lease look out especially for:

(1) **The length of the lease remaining.** The longer the better for investors.

(2) Not only the **amount of rent** being paid currently, but **when is it reviewed?**

(3) Is there a **Ratchet Clause** which prevents the rent being lowered?

(4) **Who pays the outgoings?** Ascertain *exactly* who pays the rates, insurance, repairs, fees, etc. You must ascertain who pays what costs to arrive at the true 'net' rent. Frequently some running

costs are overlooked and are the landlord's responsibility, e.g. management fees, valuers' fees, water charges, and repairs to the exterior of the building.

(5) **Rights of renewal** — Is the lease a long one straight through e.g. 10 years, and how much is remaining? Some people get muddled up with the difference between a lease of (say) 2 x 2 x 2 x 2 x 2 (total: 10 years) and a straight 10-year lease. The former means that every two years the tenant can walk out or stay on at their option — not yours. A 10-year lease means just that. There is a huge difference between the two, and it makes a difference to the value of the property as well. Obviously a long lease is worth more because of the certainty.

(6) If there are **multiple leases** is it clearly defined how much each tenant pays of the outgoings, if at all? Often there are differences which have to be ironed out to get the true picture.

(7) Are there **personal guarantees** (PGs) from the lessees? Very important. The more the merrier. No PGs means that a tenant can walk out and who do you sue? A piece of paper?

Reading and checking the leases, and especially looking for weak points, loopholes and omissions is a big part of the Due Diligence process. Finding these errors and omissions can be very rewarding or save you from much heartache.

Example

The following is a true case I experienced. A building I purchased had one major tenant (and some minor ones). The major tenant was paying $70,000 net p.a. The rent review clause was peculiar in that it provided for the usual rent review but stated that there was no ratchet clause (pity) and that when the rent was reviewed it would not fall below $50,000 p.a. in any event. The previous ding-a-ling landlord had tried to put a bottom line on the rental. Naturally enough, the tenant was looking hard at a potential saving of $20,000 p.a. at the start of the next lease term. My valuers assured me that the current rental was correct and there should not be any drop. That's all very well, but six valuers can come up with eight opinions so nothing could be guaranteed.

What to do? I studied the lease carefully and two things stood out:

> Firstly, the lease stated that there were no carparks with that particular lease, but in fact the tenant was using a part of the carpark for his trucks and vans.
>
> Secondly, the lease stated (as many do) that at rent review time the landlord 'may' review the rent.*

The word 'may' is not 'must'. There is a world of difference between the two (as the Privy Council has confirmed). So I chose *not* to review the rent at all and remained totally silent.

This obviously infuriated the tenant who unilaterally reviewed the rent by dropping it by $20,000 p.a. and daring me to do my worst.

Steady, boys, steady.

When his lower rent cheque arrived I made no comment other than to acknowledge receipt and show an outstanding balance remaining, plus penalty interest accumulating. This went on for months interspersed with long whinging letters from the tenant which I left unanswered. If I had started answering and arguing back I was potentially starting a rent review and must follow through. By remaining silent, no review was taking place.

Cunning, eh?

Months went by, and still the lower rent arrived, and still I piled on the overdues and penalties. But the bank account wasn't looking too healthy, so something had to be done to bring it to a head.

Back to the carpark question. I finally wrote to the tenant, without mentioning rent at all, and ordered his vehicles out of the carpark permanently.

*This has been recently changed in the new (2002) version of the Auckland District Law Society lease. You can change it back to 'may' if you wish.

Of course the explosion could be heard for miles. Lawyers' letters arrived by the dozen, threats flew in all directions. The upshot was that I allowed him indefinite but casual use of the carpark at no charge, while the rent remained un-reviewed at its original level.

That suited me fine.

Advantages and disadvantages

Commercial property versus residential — which is the better? Each has its own distinct advantages and disadvantages. Commercial has generally a **higher return** than residential, as well as having **easier day-to-day management** with a **better class of tenant** — sometimes but not always.

Residential on the other hand, can produce **more rapid capital growth**, and is far **more liquid** — easier to realise if money is needed in a hurry.

One of the problems with commercial is if a tenant vacates, the property can sit around empty for a long time. If you have a mortgage, that can send you broke. Hence residential, which is rarely empty, carries less risk from a cash flow and security perspective.

That is why banks love lending up to 90% or more on residential investments but rarely lend past 75% for commercial, which is a pain.

In the next chapter we will look at how to increase the value of commercial property and not rely on inflation to do it, as well as the specific types of commercial in more detail.

19.

Commercial & industrial — Part 2

Types of commercial tenants

Retailers

If ever there was a test for your nerves in the commercial property market, retail tenants are it.

Retailers are the biggest bunch of whining and whinging losers an investor can ever have the misfortune to be landed with. Occasionally you do land a good one. In that event you serenade him (or her) with flowers and song, light candles at their shop door, and pray every night for their continued good health in all weathers. The good ones are rare indeed. The rest should be lashed every morning and evening in revenge for the agony they inflict on you — the poor defenceless landlord.

Now, I might be exaggerating a little here, but really, retailers are a breed unto themselves and have to be treated quite differently from other types of tenants. Retailers are in fact little different from residential tenants, but burdened with a big dollop of extra stress.

When dealing with a retailer, bear these stresses and strains in mind and make allowances. Just think about it for a moment. Having to stay open six if not seven days a week for up to 15 hours a day is no joke. Relying on passing trade, standing around for hours with nothing happening, forced to be nice to every loony customer. It would drive the sanest person to hell and back.

But retail investments have one big advantage: they are rarely empty for long.

There is an endless supply of masochistic folk who have convinced themselves that opening a shop is an instant path to endless wealth and happiness. These poor souls learn the hard way that ninety percent of them will fail within three years. Now that's too bad, but to you, being an investor wanting only the rent, it doesn't matter a rat's backside whether they succeed or fail so long as they pay the rent in the meanwhile.

It follows that the lease is hardly worth the paper its written on as it rarely goes the distance. The chances of fresh opportunities, earlier rent increases, and endless chances to have another crack at getting better terms can be very tempting, especially when compared to dull long-term leases going nowhere.

Of course, management is much harder. It's not everyone's cup of tea to be out there beating the daylights out of retail tenants. Many investors just want a steady income stream with no problems. If that's what you prefer that's fine. I prefer the challenge.

There are other advantages (and pitfalls) to being a retail landlord as some of the following examples will demonstrate:

One of the dumbest retailers I ever came across ran a successful restaurant which had been on the same site for over 15 years. His lease ran out and he asked for a new lease. A very routine request, which required a standard response from me. After a cursory study I determined that a rent increase of $25 per week was in order, not much more than one meal, and I wrote a letter accordingly.

The response I received from my suggestion was amazing. The phone exploded in my ear. I was called every name that ever existed, my parentage was disputed, followed up by dark threats of disembowelment and imminent strangulation.

Now this is not new for me, especially from retailers. I fully expected that reason would return given a few days. Nobody could be so stupid as to throw away a lease, a business and 15 years of goodwill. A week or two later when I heard no more I took a drive to the premises and to my amazement I found that the tenant had gone, leaving everything virtually intact and in place.

My feelings of euphoria were hard to describe. I had just been handed a fully equipped and modern restaurant, which only required some basic bits and pieces to be fully operational again.

It took exactly one week to sell the business to somebody else, obtaining a good price for the fittings and fixtures, plus a substantial goodwill sum despite being closed.

But wait —there's more:

I got $100 per week more rent as well.

Them's the breaks.

There have been nasty experiences as well — so it's not always a bed of roses. For instance, there was the jewellery store tenant who fell on hard times despite it being rumoured that he was a paid-up member of the Mafia. The rates were unpaid and when that happens the City Council concerned comes back to the owner to get the money. I innocently thought that a small visit to his shop would sort matters out.

On entering the shop, there was my Mafioso friend with rings sparkling on each finger, hair slicked back, gold dangling off each wrist and the obligatory heavy gold chains around his neck. Any one of them would have paid the rates for several years.

"Now then, Alfonso," I said (for that was his name). "I have come to see you about the unpaid rates."

It was the plump lady who saved me that day. It was on her that I fell as I was hurled bodily into the street. Amidst a tangle of shopping bags and hair curlers, accompanied by blood curdling screams (mine) I vividly remember staring up from this prone position. Alfonso stood over me, fists clenched, teeth bared, flecks of foam around his mouth.

"I Smash-a You Face!! I Cut-a You Throat!! I Break-a You Legs!!" he roared.

From this I suspected that he was in a bad mood.

Being a devout coward, I took large and rapid backwards steps to my car, tearing up the rates demand as I went and offering profuse apologies in broken Italian.

He didn't get away with it. One month later he sold the business, thus requiring my consent as landlord to the Assignment of Lease. That consent cost him plenty, and this time he paid up like a lamb.

Office tenants

We now come to a completely different breed of tenant. The office tenant is one of a white collar, hard working, stress-ridden profile where image is everything. Owning offices requires a different approach as landlord. Office tenants, by their very nature and calling, are brittle at the best of times, so handle them with kid gloves.

You are facing a better class of enemy.

With the rapid change in technology in the past few years, the requirements of office space are now quite altered. Computers rule the world and offices have to be computer-friendly. More light, more power outlets, better air conditioning, higher quality fittings, carpets, drapes, and decor. Spaces are configured on lines that would have been downright inconvenient only ten years ago. Security and safety must be higher, parking better, services improved, and of course better access for disabled people. All this is costly to both tenant and landlord, yet there is one strange thing: office rentals in New Zealand are at third world joke levels.

Therefore if you invest in office space you have two choices:

(1) Get the best hi-tech space possible for those tenants willing to pay top dollar, or

(2) Get cheap rundown space.

The latter can be quite profitable as there is an endless supply of cheap rundown tenants looking for cheap rundown space. All sorts of small businesses are content with cheap space, so with a coat of paint and no frills you should have few vacancies.

Of course, at this level the ugly tenants rear their heads again. The non-payers, the grizzlers and the absconders. Fortunately, you rarely get threatening or the smash-and-run types as can be found in the retail sector.

Should you get stuck with a large amount of office space, it can be very profitable to cut it up into small offices and have a number of small businesses where one existed before. Sure, the management is a hassle, but it's better than nothing.

But be warned: there are some strange types out there and a firm hand is needed. I remember one tenant in particular who was a professional accountant and ran a busy practice.

So busy, in fact, that he didn't pay the rent (and that will never do!)

Countless letters and reminders passed between us but the rent remained unpaid, or severely in arrears. He was always pleasant (as was I) when we communicated it, but it was all done through gritted teeth.

Eventually enough was enough, and after due deliberation I tried a novel approach.

I had a good friend who was well over 6 feet tall, weighed 18 stone, with hands the size of dinner plates, a boxer's broken nose and cauliflower ears. (Which only goes to show that looks aren't everything, as he had never boxed in his life.) When he walked down the street, dogs backed away into rubbish bins and birds dropped dead out of the sky.

But he had the steel nerves I needed.

I sent him over to the accountant to have a 'chat' on my behalf, friendly-like of course. I let him take what action he thought fit — so long as he succeeded.

His technique was brilliant. After getting introduced to the accountant/tenant and while explaining the situation, it appears that he fiddled with an ornamental vase and (ahem) accidentally dropped it — smashing a glass coffee table in the process.

While trying to apologise for that accident, several pictures mysteriously fell off the wall (ahem). As he was picking these up some plants were tipped over, spilling earth and leaves over the new carpet (ahem, ahem).

Oh dear, some people are very clumsy, aren't they?

But he must have done something right.

The rent was paid on time from then on.

Industrial tenants

Once more, we have a different class of tenant. If you want trouble-free investment, with the maximum return and minimum fuss, then invest in factories, warehouses and the like. On the whole, these tenants are practical, not fussy, down-to-earth types who will fix things themselves rather than bother you, stay for long periods of time, pay their rent and outgoings, and accept reasonable rent increases with hardly a murmur.

It's also dead boring investing. Factories and warehouses are what you fit retired farmers into. No thinking required.

If you like this type of investment, just ensure that the basics are there. Good high stud, wide doors, easy access, good parking, room for trucks, easy maintenance materials, close to rail and motorway. Keep away from small industrial pockets as they can stay vacant for long periods. Stay where all the other factories are.

Also as mentioned earlier, avoid speciality buildings and buildings that have all sorts of special features built into them. Should it become vacant you will have a big headache getting it ready for another tenant who has a different business.

Either that or ensure that any tenant that wants to do specialised alterations to the property will be obliged to return it to its original state if they go.

Keeping in touch

It is necessary from time to time to visit your tenants, firstly just to show them you care (a bit) and secondly to check the property out.

As this exercise inevitably ends up with you in a very bad mood, I suggest you time these visits on certain days only. I make it a habit of doing the rounds on the days when I wake up grumpy and tired for one reason or another. This way you will be grumpy and tired all day long.

Don't spoil what could have been a good day by visiting whinging whining tenants just waiting to pounce on you with long lists of complaints.

20.

Commercial & industrial — Part 3

Increasing the value

As we learnt earlier, commercial property is valued on logic and fundamentals, with only a smidgen of emotion involved.

This fact is not only its greatest strength, but its greatest weakness. The strength lies in the certainty that facts are facts, and if one does one's homework to a reasonable standard an investment into commercial property will almost always give good returns. The trouble with this sort of logic is that it aids mightily those who understand the system and use this rigidity to gain advantage.

So be it. ***All's fair in love and war.***

The main aims of everyone who invests in commercial property are to:

(a) Get a good return

(b) Increase that return

(c) Increase the value (i.e. capital gain), thus increasing the security and future profits.

The main aim of the smart investor is to short-cut the waiting time and reap greater returns, plus capital gains, in the shortest possible time.

I agree wholeheartedly with that.

Take no notice of those who whimper and whine away about long-term goals. Many financial planners love this sort of limp-wristed phraseology and for one good reason: They want to keep you on their books for as long as possible.

Financial planners are a recent blot on the investment landscape, useful only for investors with three-inch cavity skulls who can just manage to put a spoon to their mouths.

Don't let them tell you what to do with your money. Remember they're not in the game for their health. They are using your money for one reason only: to pay themselves fat fees while you take the risk.

Remember: You want the biggest returns, the fastest capital gain and the most profits in the shortest possible time.

Financial planners won't tell you how to do that. It wouldn't pay them to have you make a quick buck because then you wouldn't need them. Recent history shows only too clearly that financial planners are just as good as anyone at stuffing things up and losing your money.

And there will be more losses to come.

For years these whiz-kids kept shoving down our throats their theory that a 'diversified share portfolio' was the only way to go. Why accept a boring 10% return from a property when you can make ten times as much at the push of the button?

"Buy shares," they cried. "Property is a waste of time," they decreed. Even the last Governor of the Reserve Bank of NZ, Dr Don Brash, once implied that property was an unproductive investment and people would be better off renting.

If everyone did decide to rent, may I ask: from whom shall they rent?

After a decade of gorging at the trough we are now witnessing the world stockmarkets sliding slowly but steadily into the abyss. Your financial whiz-kids are now strangely quiet. As their (mis-)managed share investments bleed red ink, frustrated investors are counting their losses.

That's why property is still a winner — you won't wake up in the morning with someone else telling you what your investment is worth. History and experience prove that land and buildings are worth the same today as yesterday and very likely more tomorrow, next week or next year. (Apart from some dumb investments into cheap apartments or speculative building ventures.)

Property is one of the very few investments that will pay you a rent while it sits on the shelf waiting to be eventually sold. There are very few other investments that pay as you wait and even provide a capital gain.

Do you want to know how to make extra profits out of property?

Well then, just draw up real close and listen to Uncle Olly.

Here's how you *really* do it.

Yields and how to use them

The 'yield' from a commercial property is the return or cash flow expressed as an interest rate on the total cash invested in order to purchase that investment.

In other words, using a simple model, a $1 million property returning $100,000 rent p.a. net (note net!) is showing a yield of 10%.

Put another way: What would you have to pay to purchase a property returning (i.e yielding) $100,000 p.a. net if the yield was 10%?

The answer is the same: $1 million.

But the yield can be changed at the flick of the wrist. Who says it has to be 10%? Why not 9%? Or 8% or 11% for that matter?

Usually valuers will advise on a suitable yield. But *they* rely on evidence from prior sales made by investors, who buy and sell using advice from valuers, who rely on evidence from investors etc … and around we go in an endless loop.

Just look what happens if you alter the yield:

> \$100,000 net rent ÷ 10% = value \$1 million (i.e. our basic model)
>
> \$100,000 net rent ÷ 9% = value \$1.11 million (an increase of \$110,000 — a good start)
>
> \$100,000 net rent ÷ 8% = value \$1.25 million (an increase of \$250,000 — even better!)

or how about:

> \$100,000 net rent ÷ 11% = value \$909,000 (a *decrease* in value of \$91,000 over the model at 10%)

In other words, by manipulating the yield, you can increase or decrease the value of a property with a stroke of the pen. **Same property, same rent, different value.**

If you want to be a smart investor you will have the following aims when buying or owning a commercial property:

(1) **Get the rent increased** one way or the other. (Higher rents = higher value (not to mention higher income)

(2) **Get the yield down** as much as possible because as we see in the exercise above, the lower the yield, the higher the value.

(3) Use the higher value to **refinance to pull out cash** and buy more investments — or sell on for a profit, whichever you choose.

Some tricks of the trade

There are many ways you can affect the yield and hence the value and here are some of them:

Have a chat to the existing tenant. If you can get a rent increase then obviously that will be reflected in an increase in the property's value. The same result can be achieved by getting your tenant to lengthen their lease, provide better guarantees or make improvements. The effect of these measures may not be more rent in the hand, but you end up with a stronger lease. A stronger lease will most likely drop the yield. A property that a valuer previously assessed at 10% could well become a 9% property. In that event hang onto your hat! Up goes the value.

Another way is to encourage your tenant to renovate the premises at their own cost. Give a rent holiday, agree to any reasonable wishes, bend over backwards. With any luck, the tenant will spend a fortune on your premises believing that the improvements belong to them. Legally that may be correct — but in practice any improvements become yours by default. Think about it.

How do you take paint away? Is it practical to lift laid carpets? How do you take out air conditioning without smashing everything?

Study your lease. In virtually all leases, if a tenant leaves they must restore the premises to their previous state at their cost (the reinstatement clause). As this is patently absurd, the improvements (plus a lower yield as a result) are yours.

Another way is to use a head lease. There is nothing to stop you having a tenant paying (say) $20,000 p.a. and you taking a head lease (a lease over the top of the existing lease) for $30,000 p.a. Provided the head lease is fair (i.e. at market rates), you will have increased the value of the property by 50%.

Warning: Some less scrupulous owners crank up the rents to crazy levels and then try to flog the property off to someone who hasn't a clue what the real rent should be. It happens all the time — so watch out.

Only recently I was offered a property which was paying $75,000 p.a. net but could be bought for $500,000. This represented a yield of 15%. Highly suspicious, but you never know.

On driving around for hours, I finally found this tumbledown warehouse with a shonky massage parlour for a tenant and an even shonkier lease. The place was in tatters, the roof was like a colander, and it was so small that if you smiled your cheeks touched the opposite walls. (How they conduct their business boggles the imagination — maybe they stick buckets on their heads and swing from the handles.)

The sellers had paid $200,000 six months earlier, (its real worth) then created the new 'dummy' lease (which probably wasn't actually even being paid) hoping to find a sucker who would believe it and cough up.

You must watch out for these as they are everywhere. If in doubt, ask for evidence of rent payments e.g. bank statements for the last twelve months as part of your Due Diligence.

There is yet another trick of the trade and that is what might be called 'subsidising' leases. This is done in order to get a higher rent (and hence enhance the value of the property).

Put simply, the landlord pays the tenant to pay more rent. Polite society calls these payments 'inducements'. In truth it is a bribe. There is nothing illegal about it, but at least you should be aware of it.

Take, for example, a situation where the tenant is paying $50,000 a year rent, making the property worth (say) $500,000, i.e. a 10% yield.

Give your tenant a loan for 'improvements' of $20,000 to be paid back interest-free over two years ($10,000 per year) together with the rent. Suddenly you have a tenant paying $60,000 p.a. rent (this should *still* be a fair market rent) and a new value of $600,000 using the same 10% yield yardstick.

Not bad arithmetic!

Lay out $20,000, get back $100,000.

That's good business in anyone's book.

One more thing: Don't be so dumb as to mention the loan in the lease. It's nobody's business but yours and the tenants.

There all sorts of variations on this theme, but the direction is always the same: *Get the rent up. Get the value up. Get the profit up.*

Achieve these goals and you will come to no harm.

Another cautionary tale

It's all very well talking about your rights (or the tenant's rights for that matter) under the terms of a lease. Just try to enforce your rights. You will soon find that the legal system is hopelessly slow, costly and impossibly inept. There is only one way to deal with problems: when trouble looms, take direct and immediate action.

Face-to-face confrontations are effective. So is locking the tenant out. That's very effective (even if not strictly legal).

Before any muesli-chewing, guitar-strumming, sandal-wearing tree-huggers reading this get excited, how's this for a story:

I leased a good quality office penthouse to a tenant who ran all sorts of businesses from it. I never could quite work out what these businesses were but he did pay the rent and that's all I cared about.

All went well for a year or so but then one day he rang me and asked for a three month rent holiday because of a "short-term cash flow difficulty." He would pay all the arrears in three months when he recovered.

I must have been going soft in the head that day but I agreed, and an exchange of letters followed setting the arrangement up. As a sign of good faith he gave me three company cheques to be banked in three months at intervals one day apart. Payment was 'guaranteed'.

Three rent-starved months later I rang him and reminded him that the cheques were now going to be lodged in the bank. My bank manager and I had been having sleepless nights and could now heave a joint sigh of relief.

"No worries, mate," my slow-paying tenant cheerily said. "They'll be as right as rain."

In went the first cheque. In went the second cheque. In went the third cheque.

Boingg!

Out bounced the first, the second and the third cheque in double-quick order. 'Account Closed!' Not even the hope of 'Present Again'.

Enraged, angry, and egged on by my fire-breathing bank manager, I storm to his (my?) luxury premises. He isn't there. His 900-kilo girlfriend is. She throws me out and locks the door. I ring for a mobile locksmith. He arrives within ten minutes. He drills out the lock. She starts screaming rape and murder. She dials 111. Sirens, heavy footsteps, and suddenly three profusely sweating policemen are standing in front of me.

"Naughty, naughty," they say in unison.

Horrors! It's *me* they are looking at — for "Disturbing the Peace!"

I show them the bounced cheques.

I show them the lease.

I point out my rights.

They fiddle with three sets of handcuffs.

I'm given ten seconds to hand back the keys — or else.

I hand back the keys.

"This is a civil matter" they say. "Take it to the Tenancy Tribunal."

"These are commercial premises, not a residential tenancy!" I cry.

They don't understand.

Somewhere in the shadows, 900 kilos stifles a laugh.

It's all too much and I flee.

It took another month to finally get the premises back and that was because the electricity got cut off. The tenant plus his 900 kilos of raw power disappeared. I never got the rent and it would have cost a fortune to drag them through court — if I ever found them.

The moral of the story is plain. **Don't give tenants credit. They pay on due date or out they go.**

21.

Doing up houses for fun and profit — Part 1

Without doubt, this is the biggest game in town.

At this precise moment, thousands of Kiwis are banging, hacking, painting, sanding and filling holes. Up and down the country, day and night, houses are being renovated by those who hope to reap vast riches from renovating a residential property.

And the truth is that they are right.

Doing up houses is one of the most profitable exercises anyone can engage in. It positively leapfrogs the queue in the wealth creation game.

Like anything else, there are some pitfalls and traps for beginners, but generally speaking it's a walk in the park.

For every hundred do-it-your-selfers busily working away, there are thousands more who are too stupid or too lazy to be bothered.

Don't get upset about it.

They are your market.

When I was growing up, boys went to woodwork or metalwork classes and got to know which way to hold a hammer. Girls went to cooking classes and learnt how to be good wives and mothers. That made perfect sense then — and should make perfect sense now.

Sadly, much of this basic and natural training has become rare. Now everyone is so PC that it's a wonder we don't have the boys learning how to look good in tutus and net stockings, and girls learning how to grow whiskers and kill spiders. The net result is that we have a vast number of people who have *no idea* what makes a property tick and will buy anything that is shiny and new-looking, never mind what's underneath.

Basing your investment strategy on this fact can be good business.

Some tips

(1) **Buy at the right price:** It is *essential* that you do your sums first — and that starts by not falling in love with the place. It bears repeating, I have seen many a renovator make the classic mistake of falling in love with a property and thereby paying too much. To assess the right price, some basic research must be undertaken to find out what similar properties that are already done up are selling for in the area. This is easily done through the agent handling the deal or from public records on the Net.

(2) **Buy in the right area:** Obviously buying in areas that are 'hot' is the way to go. If prices are too hot then buy in the areas immediately adjacent. Hot property areas are like mud pools, constantly bubbling and seething. If you find the heat too hot to take, then buy in the areas nearby as they will be the first to benefit — much like ripples spreading out in a pond.

(3) **Do not spend too much in the doing-up process:** When dealing in the cheaper end of the market in particular, the margins are very tight. Paint costs the same whether it's a major do-up or a cheap one. Likewise with many other trades and materials. Many an amateur renovator has come a cropper by overspending in a

fit of enthusiasm. There is no point in spending so much as to have the property owing you twice what its maximum selling price might be.

(4) **Start at the top when doing your sums:** A typical do-up exercise goes like this:

Estimated selling price, based on homework — (say) $300,000

Less legal expenses in and out	$5,000
Less agent's commission	$10,000
Valuer's fee	$500
Interest on 75% mortgage(s) for (say) 6 months @ 8%	$9,000
Renovation costs (say)	$25,000
Profit	$25,000
Total costs	**$74,500**

This means that you should not be paying more than around $225,500 for the property in the first place. These figures are very approximate of course but show the basic idea. Be aware that all sorts of things can push the result one way or the other. It may take longer to sell than you think. You may have to take a lower price to move on. The renovation costs may be cheaper or dearer than estimated.

One of the biggest expenses is the real estate agent's commission. Try selling it privately and see what happens. If you don't ask you don't get.

(5) **Know your buyer:** If there is one thing that you should do before starting out as a renovator, it is to realise that all house purchases are finally decided by women. Women make up 90% of the buying market. If the house appeals to women, it's in the bag.

Men don't really count, even if they say otherwise. So concentrate on doing things to the property that women love, such as nice colour schemes, pretty gardens, fancy bathrooms and kitchens (see next chapter).

Men only need a decent garage for the beloved car, a workshop (even if they never use it), space for a spare fridge to store the beer, and somewhere for the couch for when they are in the dogbox.

Renovating can not only be profitable but will provide you with a fund of stories that will keep your dinner guests entertained for years. For instance, this happened to me one time when I was pulling out a wall: As I pulled the last piece away I uncovered a long forgotten fireplace. I also uncovered at least a 1,000(!) dead and mummified birds which positively exploded out of the wall to spill across the room in a choking cloud of ancient dust, atrophied claws and feathers. For 50 years at least these birds had been falling down the disused chimney to die and pile up in the wall behind.

Oh, how I laughed at the sight.

Not so my workmen. They downed tools for an hour.

This story goes down particularly well just after the entrée has been cleared away and the main course and wines are being served.

(6) **Prior access:** Try if you can to get access to the property *before* settling. It is worth paying a premium because it will save heaps of cash if you can do it up before you pay. Empty houses are naturally the best target, so when making your offer, try to obtain prior access for the "purpose of renovation and repair." I have managed this neat exercise many times and it saves much aggravation and cost. Failing full access prior to settlement, the next best thing is access to various rooms in the house (even if

the vendor is still in occupation). This can be a startling exercise for the vendor, but the occasional box of chocolates or bottle of wine along the way usually smoothes the path.

As a final resort, get prior access to the exterior, i.e. the garden and outside walls, roof etc. At least some of the work will be done while the bewildered vendor looks on.

In one exercise I bought a property and did up the exterior and garden. While doing that, I advertised it for sale a little tongue-in-cheek and just told callers to do a drive by. I expected that if I was lucky I would have a few people to call back when I finally got full possession. Amazingly enough, it actually *sold* from the outside — prior to my settlement — without me ever once meeting the buyer.

(7) **Surface counts:** Whatever you do, spend time and money on the surface and don't worry about the hidden things. Remember, you are on a tight budget. Every dollar should deliver the biggest bang for the bucks. Money spent on wiring and plumbing, for instance, is wasted if you cannot *see* anything as a result. Far better to spend the money on new switches and taps and too bad if they don't actually work. There is no point in being squeamish about these matters. The purchaser (and that could be you, remember) has every right, indeed a duty, to check out all these things before making a commitment. Nevertheless, it is only the surface which is seen. Most buyers are only interested in the shiny paint and chrome finish. Don't disappoint them.

(8) **Expensive houses:** If you decide to do up an upper price bracket home then all the rules change. This is not a job for the fainthearted. Upper class buyers are almost always very fussy and will examine everything with the utmost care. They will know within minutes how much you paid for the property and will be able to work out for themselves what your profit will be.

All very trying, if not embarrassing. If you decide to get into this niche market only the best will do from the top down. This is a specialist exercise and should not be tried unless you have pots of money and are prepared to spend it.

In other words, stick to cheap and seedy houses. The buyers aren't so fussy.

22.

Doing up houses for fun and profit — Part 2

Speed is of the essence

When doing up cheaper residential properties, there is only one rule to keep in mind:

Get the job done as quickly as possible.

While you dream about this colour or that, or whether the curtains should be long or short, holding costs march relentlessly on. At every tick of the clock the bank is making more and more while you make less and less. So are the insurers and the avaricious local council.

You can just see them rubbing their hands in glee. While you work, create, and worry yourself sick, they make money — regardless.

Remember, the selling price and the profit you hope to make are strictly limited. You cannot pile the holding costs on and expect to get it all back, plus profit, at the end.

Compile a flow chart from the moment you take possession and calculate your daily holding costs. Then every day *add these holding costs on to the purchase price* (plus of course the actual costs of the renovation). You will be staggered how quickly the costs climb towards your expected sale price (and even that is debatable).

Do not hesitate to dump the project and get out if it starts to get away on you. Quit, sell, cut your losses and get out. Time and again I see good, well-meaning, hard-working renovators lose their shirts because they hang on and on and on and on … until the costs swallow up the project. The only winners are the bankers.

Where to start

If you don't sell the house from the outside you might as well not start. First impressions are everything. Before even making your offer look carefully at the outside, and the neighbours — indeed the whole street. Take lots of photographs or videos and study them at leisure. Decide what can be done to make the exterior appealing.

And whatever you do, keep the neighbours in mind. There is no point in doing up the property you are interested in if there is a run-down dogbox next door.

One of my better projects had just that sort of trouble. The house I was interested in was excellent material — but next door was a nightmare. Overgrown hedges, old cars up on blocks, bottles and rubbish everywhere. It was so grubby that the dogs buried their bones inside.

Looking up the owner was easy enough. It turned out that next door was rented out (what else?) The owner had been beaten into submission under the relentless pressure of the natural enemy of the property owners (the tenant). I volunteered to clean his property up for nothing — an opportunity he grabbed with both hands and feet.

It cost me around $500 to tidy up his grounds, trim his hedges, cart away the rubbish and water-blast the exterior (much to the astonishment of the occupants who, like most lazy tenants, seemed to thrive on dirt and rubbish).

That little exercise may have cost me $500 but it added at least $15,000 to the value of my project. Money well spent indeed.

The roof

If the roof is made of corrugated iron or metal tiles then paint it quickly. Nothing makes a worse impression then a flaky roof. There is no need to paint every part of the roof, only those parts you can see. Concentrate on what you can see and save money on the rest.

If you can't see it, neither can anyone else.

If the roof leaks (indicated by stains on the ceiling or carpets) do not let a plumber talk you into a new roof (as he surely will try to). Instead, get him to gunk up the holes and then paint over them.

As I mentioned earlier, larger holes can be covered with bits of old shirt and painted over as well. Believe me, these patches will last longer than the roof!

Gutters and downpipes

For some reason the sight of rusty and broken gutters and downpipes drives potential buyers into a turn-off tizzy. It pays to inspect these carefully as they stick out more than a leaky roof.

It was during one of these inspections that I almost ended up in the emergency ward.

I had been warned that there was a large dog on site but was assured that it was harmless as it had been tied up to a running lead (a long wire stretched across the ground from which actual the dog lead runs, allowing the dog more freedom of movement).

With my eyes firmly fixed skywards on the guttering and while walking backwards, I didn't even see the wire until I fell over it, nearly decapitating myself in the process. As I struggled on my back in a tangle of wire, mud, and rose bushes, I looked up to see a vast set of saliva-dripping, foul smelling, fetid canines hovering just over my throat.

My trousers saved me. As I leapt over the fence, Rover (the dog's name, as I subsequently learnt), took a large chunk out of the seat of my pants, ripping them neatly from crutch to cuff.

Old biddies behind lace curtains tittered as I hopped, skipped and jumped to my car, clutching my briefcase to my private parts with the remnants of my trousers flapping around my ankles. It was not turning out to be a good day. But revenge is sweet. Rover ended up at the SPCA while I bought the property and made a thumping good profit for my pains.

When replacing guttering, use plastic guttering or pipes (forget the copper) or even used lengths from a demolition yard.

Outer walls

The answer to all faults with outer walls is *Builder's Bog*™, a pink compound available from hardware stores. It fills every hole, crack, warp, and twist with a substance that hardens harder than a banker's heart. Buy several 44-gallon drums of the stuff and use it liberally. Paint over it when it's set hard (about 10 to 20 minutes) and problem solved.

The only thing cheaper is water-blasting, which can bring astonishing results.

The garden

There are many good programmes on TV and books available on how to tart up the garden. The problem with many of these good ideas is that they are expensive and take a long time to implement. Remembering that speed is the essence, there is little point is buying seedlings and small shrubs and then waiting around for years as they grow.

Instead buy 'instant' potted colour, tidy up the garden beds, mow the lawns, trim the edges and the hedges, and splash out on a few large well-grown shrubs or even trees. Clean up dirty concrete, spread chips, pebbles, or even bark (ghastly as it is). If there is no fence or gate, ready-made palings and gates can be cheaply purchased. Throw in a pergola or two, a couple of plaster gnomes with fishing rods, a large wooden butterfly on the wall and, Hey Presto, you have something that every Kiwi longs for: perfect bad taste.

Remember: as you plant the trees, shrubs and plants always leave them in their plastic bags. They will last for months, if not years, in these bags. Should you not get the price you want, you simply tell the buyer that you intend taking your favourite plants with you. Few are willing to argue.

On settlement you will have a trailer load of shrubbery for use at your next project. Saves time and money. Likewise with any pebbles, chips or ground cover. Into the trailer they go if you are not happy with the price.

The interior

The eye of the beholder always goes from the floor to the walls, and finally the ceiling. Your renovations should follow this pattern:

The kitchen

This must appeal to the women, naturally. Even in these days of mind-numbing PC, it is the women who either fall in love with the kitchen or reject it. The men just want to see where they can put the telly and fridge. Tile, polish or parquet the floor. Put a new benchtop in — nothing too expensive — and new taps if needed. New handles and masses of clean paint everywhere. Ensure that the stove is clean or replace it with a done up second-hand one. Don't worry if no water comes out of the taps, just make sure they look good. The hot water cupboard should be *screwed shut* to ensure that it is not inspected too closely.

Don't think that this is not important! I once did up a house where the water cylinder was working but somewhat dodgy, to put it kindly. Having screwed the door shut and painted the top of the cylinder to hide the rust, I then managed to sell the house to a couple on a low-deposit deal. Soon after, the couple decided to go their separate ways — never mind their legal obligations to me. Payments due on the property stopped because she said she couldn't afford to pay me on her own. She had the gall to continue staying in the property. I was now in the business of providing free accommodation for my trouble, it seemed. Threatening legal letters followed to no avail. I was losing money hand over fist — and fast!

In desperation, I sent around the debt collectors who succeeded in throwing her out, but still not another cent was paid.

It must have been a somewhat acrimonious separation. On inspection the house was a mess with holes in every wall, windows off hinges, and the carpets stained. Mercifully, the hot water cylinder was in one piece — or so I thought.

What I had overlooked was that she still had a key.

A week later when I revisited the property with some workmen I was concerned to see water running down the drive, and the garden was a sea of mud. Yet it hadn't been raining for weeks. The #%$#@ had apparently gone back in (no signs of forced entry so who else?) and quietly ripped the water pipe out of the rusty cylinder — leaving the water to pour out across all the floors, through to the basement and in every room. Walls sagged, doors jammed, carpets floated away and the smell had to be experienced to be believed!

The police could do nothing without evidence and the insurance fought every step of the way to resist paying.

One small comfort — it got rid of the cockroaches.

The bathroom

Straight after the kitchen comes the bathroom as a high priority. Cover the floor with the best and cheapest covering or tiles. Likewise, paint the walls or tile them if you can afford it. Luxury bathrooms pay big dividends. Again nice taps, forget the plumbing. Pay attention to the toilet. Women especially cannot bear grotty toilets. (Men don't care, for obvious reasons.) Install a new toilet pan and lid, and even a new cistern if required. At the very least, clean them thoroughly. Put a blue tablet in the cistern. It all gives the impression of cleanliness even if the bacteria count is actually in the billions.

Put up a fancy mirror, a pretty cake of soap, frilly curtains, a nice towel or two. It is even worth getting those plastic bands that state "this has been cleaned" and tying them around the hand basin and toilet. Women love it — and don't forget, it is they who make the final decision.

The bedrooms

It is all very well getting ideas out of books or from TV on how to change bedrooms from boring to exciting. You should note that in all cases they are displaying furnished rooms which are a completely different kettle of fish from an empty room. Forget the fancy colours and pop-art.

Paint all the bedrooms one colour — usually chicken-coop cream is quite adequate. In fact, paint the whole interior in one colour. Nothing looks worse than every room painted a different colour.

Leave that to the new owner.

More important than a fancy paint job is to try to create an extra bedroom or two. A three bedroom house is worth at least 20% more than a two bedroom house, while a four bedroom is worth 20% more again. To create extra bedrooms, look carefully at the other rooms. Is that dining area really needed? Can that sun porch be converted? Is there an old-fashioned wash house that can be converted to a spare bedroom? If possible, at least two bedrooms should be done up with the women in mind. Any extra bedrooms can have posters, and naughty pictures pinned up to suggest that the male of the species has a few rights left.

Talking of bedrooms, a word of caution: When inspecting a property *always knock* on a bedroom door before entering — even if you were assured that the property was vacant. On many an occasion as I have been inspecting a property I have blundered into a bedroom only to find two (and sometimes more) lovebirds quite unaware that anyone else was in the house. One can have one's face rearranged by angry lovers interrupted in the middle of a steam-driven horizontal tango.

I recall one such episode when I was tiptoeing around a property and carefully knocking on all the doors as I went, just in case. After a thorough examination of the interior, I was certain I was alone. I then stepped through the french doors to look at the rear garden.

Good heavens, what was this? There, lying sunbathing on the deck, were two totally beautiful (and totally naked) young women who could easily have stepped out of the centrefold of a girlie magazine. As I slowly took in the situation (why hurry?) I realised that they had not yet noticed me. Both wore eye shades and head phones playing at full volume (all right — so they weren't quite naked).

But what was this? Curses! Beyond them a huge naked mountain of beer belly and hair slowly sat up and eyed me ferociously. I could see the flames licking around his nostrils as he staggered onto his feet and lurched towards me.

"I've only come to read the meter," I lied, as I knee-trembled backwards through the french doors.

Thank goodness he was drunk. As I ran at full speed through the house back to my car, he slipped on the top step and fell belly-first all the way down to land on his naughty bits which verily did pain him sorely.

Thus, dear reader, did I escape his wrath, for had he caught me, I would surely have never been able to write this book.

The floors

Although the floors are extremely important, try to get away from any expensive finishes. If the floors are wooden, have them polished and varnished (with polyurethane). This looks great and costs little.

If the carpet is good, have it properly stretched and cleaned. If the carpet is only good in parts, polish or re-carpet the bad areas, and use the good carpet to finish off the remainder. If all else fails, there are firms that sell first-rate new (but slightly flawed) or used carpet.

If the floors are wonky and sloping through age, leave them alone. An under-house repiling job costs more than it's worth. Just say that sloping floors are part of the charm of older homes.

As a last resort, buy large carpet squares or rugs. They will cover a multitude of sins (and better still, can be taken away for next time!)

Ceilings

Paint flat white and forget.

Garaging

If there is a carport, enclose it with a roller door and walls. Security is a big plus and adds ten times its cost to the overall value. If there is no garaging, erect a carport. The man of the house must keep his car dry at all costs.

Overall decor

Never partially furnish a house you are trying to sell. It looks pathetic and sad. Either it should be totally empty but fresh and newly painted, or it should be fully furnished. I know of many renovators who have house lots of furniture that they cart from place to place — right down to the plastic flowers, kettle, crockery, toaster, and magazines. If you have the room to pay and store a full house lot it's a marvellous way to sell a property.

If it's not practical, then leave the house empty.

Renovating is a doddle if you keep in mind the one secret: Speed.

Alternatively, if the budget cannot stand the strain, then live in the house yourself and do it up around you. It is a ghastly way to exist (and hard on the family) but at least this way you save on rent or interest living somewhere else.

23.

Don't believe everything you see or hear

As we have discussed, the property market is, by its nature, fraught with danger and traps for the unwary. Even the cheapest real estate runs to thousands of dollars if not millions.

As a consequence, all sorts of dubious deals are done by people who have no scruples or morals whatsoever.

Here are some of the more tricky things to watch out for:

The 'Spoiler'

One of the most popular tricks of the trade is for a ruthless property investor to get in the way of some else's deal and then blackmail one or both parties. In return for a large fee, they will 'go away'.

These sort of people are a curse on the market. Many have come a cropper when they have picked on the wrong parties. Nevertheless they still keep popping up, so there is obviously money in the game.

Here's an example in which I was personally involved:

I had the job given to me to assist in the private selling of a town house from a deceased estate. The vendors were all very emotional, as can be imagined, and couldn't face real estate agents or marketing programs. They asked me to word an advertisement and show any prospective buyer through the property on their behalf.

Because I knew the family well I as only too happy to assist (for no charge of course).

The advertisement must have been a good one, because there was a flurry of replies and several offers were presented almost immediately.

To do the right thing by all concerned the best offer was accepted. As it was conditional, a second unconditional offer was also accepted as a back-up.

The second offer would only become binding if the first offer fell over. This is normal practice and the second offer was carefully written up, clearly stating how and when it would come into force, if at all.

The first offer became unconditional and so the back-up purchaser was advised that they had missed out.

You would think that was the end of the matter but it wasn't. Unbeknown to me the back-up man was a 'Spoiler' looking for easy pickings.

This character, realising that he was dealing with a deceased estate where people's emotions are very brittle, decided that this deal would be a soft target.

His solicitor was the first to strike with a formal demand disputing the cancellation. The property belonged to his client, he claimed. His bogus demand centred around whether or not the offer from the Spoiler had been properly lapsed when the first offer became unconditional.

It was all rather technical, but thoroughly bogus nevertheless. How the solicitor acting for the Spoiler could lower his ethics to this extent will always remain a mystery to me.

Worse was to follow. On the strength of this bogus claim, a caveat was lodged on the property's title. This caveat prevented any dealing whatsoever with the property until the matter was resolved.

Now we were in a nice pickle. The genuine buyers started screaming to settle. Their solicitor climbed into the act. If settlement didn't take place on the due date damages would arise. The vendors, under enough stress as it was, were virtual basket cases.

The Spoiler threatened to enforce his rights through the courts. It would take months, perhaps years, to sort it out.

In a blind rage I did the only thing left to do. I called on the Spoiler personally, bailing him up at his workplace in front of his colleagues.

There is nothing like a bit of face-to-face confrontation to loosen things up.

Then the truth came out. For the sum of 'only' $30,000 he would drop his claim.

So that was it! Blackmail pure and simple.

It was the threat to take the matter to the Law Society that did the trick. The solicitor who handled the Spoiler's file knew it was a rip-off and pulled the plug.

It still cost $6000 in legal fees to get the matter settled, which left a very sour taste in everyone's mouth.

Who's the dummy?

As we have discussed, when it comes to valuing a property, the difference between residential and commercial property rests on one basic principle. Residential values are based on emotion. Commercial values are based on returns.

A house appeals to a buyer because it feels 'right'. Hence, if it feels very right people will pay more and vice versa.

A commercial property goes up in value based on the yield (or rent) it produces. Of course there are many exceptions to this, but in the main the basic formula is:

R x Y = P (where R=rent Y=yield P=Price)

Therefore, 2R x Y = 2P

In simple English: **Double the rent and you double the price.**

Increasing commercial rents is not easy in non-inflationary times. But if a 'dummy' is used, it's dead easy. And this is where many an unwary purchaser has fallen in head first.

What the tricksters do is create a lease where none existed before, or perhaps where an inferior lease already exists. There are many variations on this theme, but the endgame is always the same: get the rent up somehow using any such trickery, because when the rent rises, the profits get bigger.

As a simple example, if a commercial property is producing a rent of $100,000 per annum net, then with the usual yield of 10% it should be worth $1 million.

However, if you can get the rent up to $150,000 per annum then the same property is worth $1.5 million.

Time and again I have seen jacked-up rents used to create jacked-up prices. Then, when a rent review comes along the rent falls back to the real market value, or the tenant moves out to something cheaper. Either way the value of the building drops — frequently wiping out the investor's equity.

Not a pretty sight.

Let me give you a few real life experiences which will show you some of the many ways 'Dummys' can be created.

These include:

(a) The Dummy rent guarantee (b) The Dummy tenant (c) The Dummy Head Lease.

Dummy rent guarantees

This little number is used frequently to sell off commercial property, and often residential as well.

The old saying that there's no such thing as a free lunch is only too true in this case. In virtually every situation where a rental guarantee is given, it is the *purchaser* who actually pays for their own guarantee.

In commercial or residential property it is quite common for the developer or dealer to guarantee the rent for a year or two at a certain figure. In this manner, a far higher price can be obtained with little risk to the seller.

For example: a factory is leased out at (say) $50,000 p.a. for two years. Using the 10% yield as a guide it should be worth $500,000. What the developer does is get the tenant to pay (say) $75,000 p.a. which increases the value to $750,000. They then sell it to the naive investor and pocket $250,000 extra. They then repay the tenant the $50,000 being the excess rent charged over the two year period and keep the $200,000 overpaid by the purchaser/victim.

After two years with this exercise the new owner will get a big shock when the rent falls back to $50,000 p.a. and the property drops $250,000 in value.

There are all sorts of variations possible on this theme, but the basic lesson is this: If you decide to buy, *check the rental being paid to ensure it is at market rates* — as assessed by an independent valuer.

The same applies to residential property. There are many apartments being sold where for example, the rent is guaranteed for two years. (A twist on this is an offer not to charge mortgage interest for one or two years.) All that really means is that the 'give away' is built into the price you are paying.

To test this, have an independent valuer check out the true value or rent before you buy. Better still, ask the seller what the cash price is without any guarantees. In nine cases out of ten there will be a hefty discount offered. This discount is what you are paying to buy your own guarantee.

The dummy tenant

This applies mainly to commercial property, especially those with multiple tenancies. Say you are looking at an investment with four tenancies, but you notice one of the spaces seems empty. The seller hands you a lease for the empty space which shows that ABC Ltd has entered into a lease for that space and will be moving in shortly.

Make sure that ABC Ltd actually exists (and that the persons signing exist) before committing yourself. What sometimes happens is that after settlement ABC Ltd vanishes, leaving you with empty space as well as an unpleasant drop in income and value!

I had this experience not so long ago. While considering a commercial property, I was given the lease documents. All seemed in order, other than that the space was empty. To reinforce matters, I was also given photocopies of previous rent payment cheques, plus full details of the tenants.

Fortunately, I checked matters out and found to my chagrin that the company had been *struck off* 12 months earlier, and the cheque account had been *closed for two years*. In my view, it was attempted fraud but the cost and trouble involved wasn't worth it. I walked away.

Dummy head leases

Yet another variation of the same trick is played, usually with commercial property. Say a property is let at a fair market value of $50,000 p.a., creating a resale value of around $500,000. The seller takes a Head Lease over the same property for (say) two years at $75,000 per annum, pushing up the value to $750,000. They then sell the property and pay out $50,000 over two years to honour the Head Lease (while collecting the sub-tenant's $50,000 p.a. of course). At the end of the two years the Head Lease expires, leaving the multiple tenancies in the shaking hands of the investor once again — but with the worth of the property much reduced in rents and value.

The bottom line is this: **Do not believe a word of any of the leases or documents you are presented with when buying a property.** Get a second opinion from a trained independent professional before doing anything.

24.
Property syndicates

People have been coming together and forming syndicates (or partnerships or companies) since the dawn of civilization. This common method of doing business has huge advantages over sole traders. Syndication is the combined efforts of a group with a single purpose in mind: to obtain a maximum return — more than can be made by an individual — at minimum risk.

The syndication of investments is the financial engine that drives the world.

Indeed, all businesses are syndicates in one form or another. Whether a syndicate is in the form of a group of partners, or shareholders in a company, or unit holders in a trust, it is in practice all the same. Only the legal structures are different, to suit the particular type of business involved. The trillions of dollars of profits made by Microsoft, Guinness Peat, General Motors etc for the gleeful shareholders speak for themselves.

Syndication of property investments is one type of partnership with particular advantages. Usually formed by way of unit trusts (although shares in public companies and special partnerships are also common) they can bring strong and steady returns to investors with the minimum effort or risk.

To show how popular such property trusts are, just look up the listed companies and syndicates in the newspapers of the world. There are literally thousands of them. To that list can be added a thousand times more for the hordes of smaller syndicates that remain unlisted i.e. private syndicates (just like private companies).

With very rare exceptions (there have been some unfortunate outcomes from time to time) most of them continue to pour out wealth and good returns for their investors with very low risk.

Basic principles

(1) Everyone has to live somewhere

(2) Every business needs premises

(3) Everything has to be made somewhere.

These are the cornerstones of property investment — and why it is as solid as it is. Property provides somewhere to live, to work and to provide goods and services. Everything else is transient.

Profile of a typical property investment

As syndicates are risk-averse (or should be!), any property that might be considered has to have all or most of the following qualities:

(1) **Blue Chip:** Any property has to be a modern building, with sound long-term tenants providing a continuous cash stream for the investors.

(2) **Capital Growth:** Any property has to have a good chance to gain in value over time. Therefore old properties, poorly sited properties, or rents that are unsustainable are not considered.

(3) With few exceptions, there should be a **multiplicity of tenants** for added security. Any single tenant can leave, or go broke, and empty buildings provide no income. However with several

tenancies in place, even if one leaves, it is not going to be a big problem.

I have been involved in many such entities in the past, for the most part spectacularly successful (with one exception — see *Lost Property*).

Bigger is not always better — listed property syndicates

For those who want something bigger there are always the larger property syndicates of which there are many. Overseas they are big business indeed and run far more aggressively than in New Zealand.

The perceived advantages of big property syndicates are:

(1) More buying power

(2) Better quality of properties

(3) Steady dividend

(4) Shares (or units) can be publicly listed and traded

(5) Expert management

(6) Multiplicity of investments

(7) Spread of risk

(8) Security

(9) Growth and capital gain.

In reality, as far as New Zealand is concerned, most big property syndicates are a dismal failure. Their sole purpose is to make the promoters rich through excessive management fees and a guaranteed income for life.

The actual disadvantages of most New Zealand-run syndicates are:

(1) Shares or units sell well below asset backing value

(2) The costs of set-up are horrendous

(3) Management fees are a rip-off

(4) Shares or units are very slow sellers or illiquid

(5) The managers take few chances as it doesn't pay

(6) The quality of the properties is generally appalling

If you don't believe me, get a copy of a prospectus for one of the big property syndicates which are currently on offer or have been on offer in the last few years. Have a good read of them. They are all much of a muchness.

Tucked away in the fine print you will most probably find:

(a) Massive start-up fees for the promoters

(b) Huge ongoing management fees year in and year out — also for the promoters

(c) Virtually unsaleable properties that have one advantage: size (bigger size = more management fees)

(d) Appallingly bad management credentials

(e) No guarantee that you will ever be able to sell your shares or units easily on the open market

Most big syndicates are designed to make the managers fat and for the Mom & Pop investors to get as little as possible.

How a good syndicate works — a few guidelines

(1) Investments are only in main centres where demand is greatest. Maybe the yield will be lower to begin with but it will be much easier to move out of if the need arises. Trophy or flagship properties only. No dull sausage blocks. They have to not only *be* sexy but *look* sexy as well. Having secured a good property, it is then offered to members of the syndicate who are free to choose to invest in it or not.

(2) The returns should be between 7 and 10% p.a., paid monthly or quarterly. (This is virtually double current bank deposits.)

(3) Properties should be under $7 million in value and preferably under $5 million. The reason for this is that these size properties are easier to sell when the time comes. I would rather have ten $1 million dollar properties than one $10 million dollar property. It's safer and spreads thc risk. The fatal blunder some syndicates have made is to be driven more by their directors' egos than by common sense. Buying $30 million investments in provincial towns, for instance, is not a good idea. These are virtually saleproof and should the tenant leave, there is also a king-size headache to deal with.

(4) Professional, qualified managers only.

(5) Fees set at a percentage of profits. Good years, higher fees; bad years, lower fees. (Make the buggers work for their money.)

(6) Monthly dividend cheques.

(7) Bonus shares (or units) in lieu of cash.

(8) The units, shares, or proportionate ownership title that each investor holds in a particular property are freely saleable to any other person on the open market or privately.

(9) Borrowing should be non-existent or very modest. The maximum I would recommend would be 40% of value (preferably less) to be bulletproof in good times or bad. The huge equity remaining is the ultimate safeguard in case of any major downturn in the economy. Over-gearing (i.e. borrowing too much) has been the Achilles heel of many property syndicates and companies in the past.

(10) Owning the land for rent, and selling off the building, viz. being leaseholders. This means no depreciation, wear or tear.

(11) A sinking fund to guarantee buy-back of shares or units at least at cost.

(12) It is not common practice, but I think it is a good idea to have a 'sunset' clause inserted in every syndicate's rulebook. This sunset clause would state, for instance, that after ten years the property would be sold and the capital returned to the investors. Only a majority of investors in that syndicate could overturn that by voting otherwise. The majority would then buy out the minority who still wanted to sell.

(13) A policy of buying properties overseas on the same principles.

(14) An aggressive policy to buy into projects at the drawing board stage, thus buying wholesale and maximising profits.

(15) A policy of selling when a capital profit can be made.

Property syndication in New Zealand is frequently run by hucksters and wannabes. Overseas they are hugely successful and of course popular.

There is no reason that could not be the case here.

25.

Tax and the investor

Disclaimer: This chapter does not purport to be a detailed tutorial on tax law for investors. Rather, it is an introduction to some topics on which you should seek further information and formal tax advice. Also, it is written for the NZ edition of this book. Consult your tax professionals to clarify what is appropriate for you and your specific circumstances. Thanks to my editor, Peter Aranyi, for this chapter (among other things).

It is a broad principle of our tax system that expenses incurred in the generation of taxable income (or the *attempt* to do so) are deductible against that, or other, income. How does this help you as a property investor? Well, read on…

Tax deductible items & expenses

(Make sure you get receipts)

Accountancy fees — including bookkeeping costs and property management charges.

Advertising — the costs of advertising any property that you have to let. Advertising costs for the *sale* of any property can only be claimed against any taxable profits arising from a sale or against any depreciation recovered.

Bank fees — monthly activity fees, other charges, loan application fees.

Debt collection costs — credit reporting agency fees, debt collection fees, court costs, private investigator's fees etc.

Depreciation — Chattels and separate components of a building can be separated from the purchase price and depreciated at much higher rates than the building itself (see section below).

Entertainment — This covers the costs of entertaining anyone associated with your property business, e.g. real estate agents, property managers, vendors, purchasers, tenants, valuers, professional advisers etc. (You can only claim 50% of the expenditure.)

Home office expenses — A percentage of all the costs relating to your home office: power, telephone rental (landline and mobile), all business toll calls, postage and stationery, computer, fax and office equipment, photocopying, internet connection. Be reasonable.

Insurance costs — house, contents, mortgage repayment, even term life insurance (if it is a requirement of the mortgage lender).

Lawyers' fees — Legal fees (other than finance-related fees) connected with the purchase of the property should be capitalised as part of the property cost (and depreciation claimed). Legal costs, court fees, caveat registration fees, lease preparation, guarantees, etc are claimable as expenses.

Motor vehicle expenses — Including registration, insurance, repairs, mileage for any trip that is related to generating income from your rental property, i.e. trips to and from the property, to the bank (to check the rent, arrange loans), to see your professional advisors, showing tenants, etc. These are claimed based on the proportion of business use shown in a logbook (ugh!), which you must keep for three months every three years.

Rates — Rates paid on investment property are tax-deductible (when paid by the owner! When tenants pay, it's *their* expense.)

Repairs & maintenance — Painting, plumbing, carpet cleaning, electrical and stove repairs, builders, lawnmowing, landscaping, gardening (see note below about the difference between Repairs and Improvements).

Seminars, meetings, conferences and training costs — course fees, travel, accommodation and related costs.

Subscriptions and research — Magazines, journals, newsletters and the newspaper are all deductible (including the purchase costs of this book!) if you currently own investment property or are seeking an investment.

Travel and accommodation — The costs of any travel and accommodation associated with your investment may be claimed. (Be reasonable, the tax people look hard at this area.)

The distinction between *repairs & maintenance* and *improvements*

Why it's important:

Repairs & Maintenance are treated as an *expense* item — therefore claimable against income (reducing your tax bill), whereas an improvement must be *capitalized* and only a portion of the cost claimed each tax year as Depreciation.

Accountants will tell you there's a fine line between expenditure that improves an asset (capital), and expenditure that restores an asset (expense). Typically, the onus of proof falls on the taxpayer to justify their claim for repairs and maintenance if questioned by the tax department.

Guidelines:

An improvement makes something better than what previously existed: alterations, additions, replacements, reconstruction with superior materials, extensions — or a combination of these.

A repair is defined as restoring/maintaining an asset in a condition close to its original state.

General rule:

If the expenditure increases the useful life of the asset, its output or efficiency, then it could be classed as an improvement.

(Note that just because a property may have a greater value as a result of 'repairs' it does not automatically follow that these 'repairs' are an 'improvement'.)

Repairs or improvements: the acid tests

Timing: was the repair needed at acquisition to enable the property to be rented? Or was it fit for the purpose at acquisition? Repairs carried out at a later date, to enable the property to continue to be used for that purpose, are deductible.

Price adjustment: was the property bought at a bargain price to compensate the purchaser for essential repairs? If so, the repairs may well be classified as improvements.

Modern-day equivalent *vs* superior materials: Using 'modern-day equivalent' materials to repair outdated materials (e.g. replacing scrim with gib board as room lining) is considered repairs. Using a 'superior' material compared to a 'modern-day equivalent' of the original material may result in your repair being classified as an improvement.

As this summary has demonstrated, this is a technical, tricky area. Rely on your tax professional to guide you — and get their advice before you act. Something as simple as an additional, appropriately worded clause in your Sale and Purchase Agreement can save you tax.

Depreciation — phantom losses

Depreciation is one of the advantages that property investment has over almost every other form of investment. The tax department allows you to claim a percentage of the value of your assets (land excluded) each year against your income from those assets as depreciation, on the basis that they are wearing out each year.

The tax department gives you an allowance for these items and you can claim this 'phantom' expense each year, reducing your taxable income.

The crunch comes when you sell the asset and discover that in fact, unlike your computer or car, commonly your real estate hasn't gone down in value — just the opposite. 'Depreciation clawback' or 'depreciation recovered' is regarded as income in the year of the sale through a formula based on the difference between the book value of your asset and its sale price.

This is a topic whose detail is beyond the aim of this chapter, but suffice to say that as a investor you *must* make yourself aware of the advantages of depreciation and what it can do for your cash flow. At its very worst, claiming depreciation is like getting an interest-free loan from the government.

Depreciation can be calculated and claimed using two methods: either *straight line* or *diminishing value* (talk to your accountant about the difference).

Broadly, you can choose one of three approaches:

(1) **Claim no depreciation on anything** — the least complicated, but of no benefit.

(2) **Standard depreciation** — depreciate the building at a low fixed rate and the basic chattels (stove, floor coverings, light fittings, fixtures & fittings) at a somewhat higher rate.

(3) **Accelerated depreciation** — hire a chattels valuer to individually assess the value of everything in the property that could possibly

be removed, including burglar alarms, extractor fans, towel rails, letterbox, garage doors and remote openers, fences and decks, electrical wiring, hot water cylinder, plumbing, spa, non-load-bearing walls, TV aerials, gas heaters/woodburner etc.

The valuer will create a detailed report and schedule of these chattels which, as a result, can be depreciated at (much higher) individual rates published by the tax department. You will not believe the additional depreciation you can claim!

Remember, depreciation clawback has no time limit (contrary to some uninformed advice). So, in the year of sale or transfer of the asset you must enter the difference between the book value of the asset and the price you got for it on sale as *income* in your tax return. Some accountants suggest not claiming depreciation to prevent building up this future 'liability'. Ask yourself this: why *wouldn't* you want an interest-free loan from the government?

Legal structures for owning investment property

The topic of ownership structures for property investors is not an area where 'one size fits all.' As we have discussed, purely from the point of view of asset safety, it makes sense to compartmentalise your affairs with different legal entities for different types of investing.

That is, hold your long-term investment (buy & hold) property in a separate legal entity to any speculative (buy & flick) or trading (rent-to-buy or wraps) deals.

It can also be very tax-efficient to create an arrangement of interlinking entities that can relate to each other.

Seek competent professional advice on these matters and be prepared to pay for it. Leave the finer details to the professionals — *your primary job as an investor is to find and negotiate the deals* — but make sure you have a decent understanding of the arrangements. If ever there was an area where it is important to pay attention, this is it.

How you hold your property depends on a number of factors:

(1) How concerned you are about asset protection from creditors in another part of your life

(2) Whether you are an investor (buy & hold) or a speculator/trader (buy & flick), or developer (buy, improve & flick)? (see earlier chapter)

(3) Whether you plan to do any development or subdivision

(4) Your need for tax management

Broadly, your options are:

(1) **Direct ownership** — either sole trader or partnership

Don't even think about this for investment property! Banks love direct ownership because it's so simple to understand, but it only makes sense if you're putting the property in your (non-investing) child or spouse's name to isolate it from your own affairs.

(2) **Limited liability company** (including LAQC)

These are highly favoured by accountants and many investors. They are relatively cheap and easy to form. A company creates a separate legal and tax entity which has considerable flexibility to distribute income, can employ shareholders, and can easily transfer ownership by way of shares to other family members.

Of course, there's no free lunch and the compliance and administration costs of a company need to be paid. Another factor is that losses incurred within the company (even phantom losses created through depreciation claims) must stay within the company as 'losses carried forward' to be deducted from future profits.

The **Loss Attributing Qualifying Company** (LAQC) is a special vehicle which overcomes this limitation. An LAQC can pass losses out to its shareholders in proportion to their shareholding, allowing those losses to offset other taxable income. In return for this privilege, the shareholders (no more than 5) must each personally guarantee to the tax department any future income tax liabilities of the LAQC.

(3) **Family Trust or Trading Trust**

For many investors, trusts are a favoured option — either a family trust with individual trustees (people) or a trading trust (which often has a limited liability company acting as trustee).

A modern, flexible trust offers you the ability to control property while having no ownership in it. This gets your assets out of harm's way should the wheels come off one of your enterprises. A trust can relate as a separate entity to other legal entities or individuals. It can distribute income or capital to a wide range of beneficiaries with much more flexibility than a company.

The disadvantages are increased paperwork, administration and compliance costs, a genuine loss of immediate control if you involve an independent or professional trustee, and added complexity when dealing with lenders. Most lenders will demand a personal guarantee from the trustees — limited to the assets of the trust.

Take it seriously

Seek advice, read books, and talk to other investors about their structures. This is a vital area for property investors and not to be taken lightly. If you're trading, dealing or developing property, pay attention to the issue of 'tainting' where these activities carried out by one entity can adversely affect the tax treatment of another.

Fixing mistakes in your legal structures after the fact can be expensive — and can act as a red flag to the tax department.

To repeat once more: Seek competent professional advice (from professionals involved in property investing) on this vital area.

26.

Closing thoughts

Why property? What is it about real estate that grabs you by the throat and won't let go? I have asked myself that question many times and the answer is never easy. It is a combination of profit, security, gambling and ego.

Let me put this way: what are the advantages and disadvantages of property as an investment or speculation?

Advantages

(1) Even with the cheapest property, you are dealing with big numbers. In my experience, people spend $100,000 as quickly as $1000. Why wait a 100 times longer for a profit?

(2) Security is a big issue. Even the meanest and most boring property is more secure than standing behind a counter selling widgets, buying shares, or banking on pyramid schemes.

(3) Banks love lending on property for the same reasons you want to buy it. They have security and stability through thick and thin. If you have the chance to borrow someone else's money at 8% and make 12%, plus the hope of capital gain, why not?

(4) What else can you buy that provides an income while you sit on it? All properties eventually sell — whether it be a month after purchase or a lifetime later. Not many other assets provide both an income and almost certain capital growth over time.

(5) There's always a chance that you can make a windfall profit in the short term. (Not to be counted on, but it *does* happen — and quite often.)

(6) Because property investment can be glacial at times, it gives you much free time in between deals. Provided you can stand the wait, this is a wonderful gift. Time is the only thing that cannot be manufactured.

(7) With this extra time you can live three lives at once: business, family, and pleasure. To echo my thoughts from Chapter 1, the poor sods who must work 9-5 six days a week and then squeeze their whole life into the dark hours or weekends are to be pitied. Thank goodness there are so many of them or the system would shudder to a halt. Working for a salary is a form of enforced slavery. What you can earn per hour is all there is. There is no more. Your whole life has to fit into that hourly rate.

(8) When you are a full-time investor you have the luxury of being able to wake up every morning and do nothing if you want to. (Don't get any ideas. In reality you have to be very self-disciplined.)

(9) The other luxury is that you know from day to day that your investment is worth more or less what it was worth yesterday — and will be worth tomorrow and next year. You will not wake up and find that some CEO had fiddled the books and the property is worth 10 cents. (Ask any sharemarket investor — they will tell you all about it.)

(10) Because the numbers can be so big, the chance to make a spectacular profit is always there. Everybody knows of a property they could have bought for $100 twenty-five years ago which is now worth $50 million. They were talked out of it at the time, and now it's too late.

But is it?

Disadvantages

There is only one: Can you go for a long periods without a regular income? If you can't bear the thought, stay in your 9-5 job. The rest of us will get on with it.

One final note

I have assumed right through this book that you want to be a property *investor*. If you want to be a *developer,* that is an entirely different game. Developers are gamblers. They buy holes in the ground, put up a building, and hope to sell it for a profit. It is heart attack country. Don't do it unless you are well-funded.

Likewise, with property *speculators* who buy today and hope like crazy they can sell for a profit tomorrow. Also heart attack country. If you can afford the occasional loss, then go for it. (All care and no guarantees.)

Finally, for people who ask me why I wrote this book and gave away so many secrets?

That's easy to answer. I did it for two reasons:

(a) An informed market is easier to do deals in all round.

(b) 99% of the population still won't have a clue about property investment and never will.

That leaves the remaining 1% of us to have all the cream.
Good luck, and happy hunting!

About the author

Olly Newland was born in Lower Hutt, grew up in Plimmerton, then Karori, Wellington and, as a teenager, in Auckland.

In his books, *The Coming Property Boom* (1978), *The Property Boom* (1981), and *Lost Property* (first edition 1994, updated 2001) he correctly foresaw many of the coming market events.

His previous books are still quoted today and are keenly sought by those seeking insight and extra knowledge in a complex and fascinating field.

Wheeling and dealing through the 1960s and '70s, Olly saw and accurately foretold the huge increases in property prices that swept the market during that period. By the late '70s he had bought and sold literally hundreds of houses.

In the '80s he founded a very successful public company, Landmark, specialising in commercial property investments. Landmark grew from $5 million to $500 million in just a few years. Along with most others, it was swept away by the cataclysmic events of 1987, which few people foresaw.

Since then he has pursued in private an active role investing in a mixture of residential and commercial properties on a long-term basis.

Olly continues to deliver seminars on property investing in association with Empower Education and offers a personal mentoring programme for a small group of people each year.

He lives in Auckland and remains married to his first wife. They have three adult children. He enjoys antiques collecting and classic cars.

Olly Newland seminars

In his more than 40 years as a full-time investor, Olly Newland has had his ups and downs. He's survived and thrived through various booms and busts, including the '87 sharemarket crash and the subsequent property slump, then boom.

Along the way, he's learned countless lessons about making the most of property investing — in any market. He's dealt with just about everything a residential or commercial landlord could expect to face — and some things no one should face!

Olly Newland offers live seminars and training courses, including his special weekend tutorial *Mastering Property Investment*™, which give you the chance to get alongside and learn from this experienced and active investor. You can learn from what he has learned. He'll share information and knowledge that is vital to your success as a real estate investor, whether residential or commercial.

For details of your next opportunity to see Olly Newland in person, and to receive a FREE audio tape about *Mastering Property Investment*™

Call 0800 37 69 37 (in New Zealand) or
+64 9 535 2415 (International)
or visit www.EmpowerEducation.com

Also by Olly Newland

Lost Property

(updated edition)

"A must-read for property and sharemarket investors. Newland's book is full of warnings and lessons to help you succeed."

Many people remember with a shudder the massive stockmarket crash around the world in 1987. In New Zealand, as in many countries, it came on the back of an unprecedented share and property boom when it seemed that huge sums of money could be made for the asking.

One of the darlings of the New Zealand scene at that time was Olly Newland, founder of Landmark, wheeler and dealer supreme. Banks virtually queued at his door to lend him money, the media for advice and comment, and he was in demand as a speaker to investor groups.

Then, beginning in New York, the market suddenly crashed.

In this book, Olly Newland gives an insider's view of the build-up and the let-down — and lays the blame firmly at the doors of banks and the government of the day. Readers may never trust either again.

In the **new updated edition** Olly Newland reflects on how little and how much has changed since the 1987 sharemarket crash. In four new chapters, he shares how it's still possible to make a respectable living from investing in property. He gives practical and up-to-date advice for those wanting to build wealth and ongoing passive income from property investing.

Published by Empower Leaders Publishing Ltd.

ISBN 0-9582307-0-6

Available from good bookstores or **www.EmpowerEducation.com**

Also by Olly Newland

Real Estate Master Class

Audio tapes

Learn property investing secrets in this exclusive live recording featuring Olly Newland and expert guest speakers.

If you're ready to move forward as a real estate investor, this brilliant tape set by Olly Newland will give you the practical tools to do it.

Recorded at one of Olly's live weekend events, *Real Estate Master Class* will give you insights into the way successful investors think — and how they approach their deals.

You can benefit from Olly's enormous experience in all aspects of real estate investing. Through these tapes he will teach you what to look for, how to judge value, how to do the numbers, deal with paperwork, and how to deal with real estate agents and tenants on your terms.

Expert guest speakers will give you advice on funding, valuation, legal, tax and ownership issues.

These tapes are full of practical, down-to-earth advice about the nitty-gritty of making money as an investor in the real world.

Available from **www.EmpowerEducation.com**

About Empower Education

EMPOWERING YOU FOR SUCCESS™
www.EmpowerEducation.com

Empower Education aims to offer the best financial education and training available and to bring you learning tools and resources that will empower you for success.

Programmes

- Real Estate, Sharemarket, & Business Success seminars and events
- 3 Hours to Freedom® Club
- Financially Free Families™
- The B.E.S.T. Business & Entrepreneurial Skills for Teens®
- Financial Academy for Youth®
- Personal development programmes

Educational resources and products

- Robert Kiyosaki's CASHFLOW® games, books and products
- Books, tapes, and software on Wealth and Finances, Business Success, and Personal Development

For more information, and news of upcoming financial education events and resources, please contact:

Empower Education Ltd
PO Box 39-115 Howick, Auckland, New Zealand
Phone +64 9 535 2415 Fax +64 9 535 2416
info@EmpowerEducation.com   www.EmpowerEducation.com

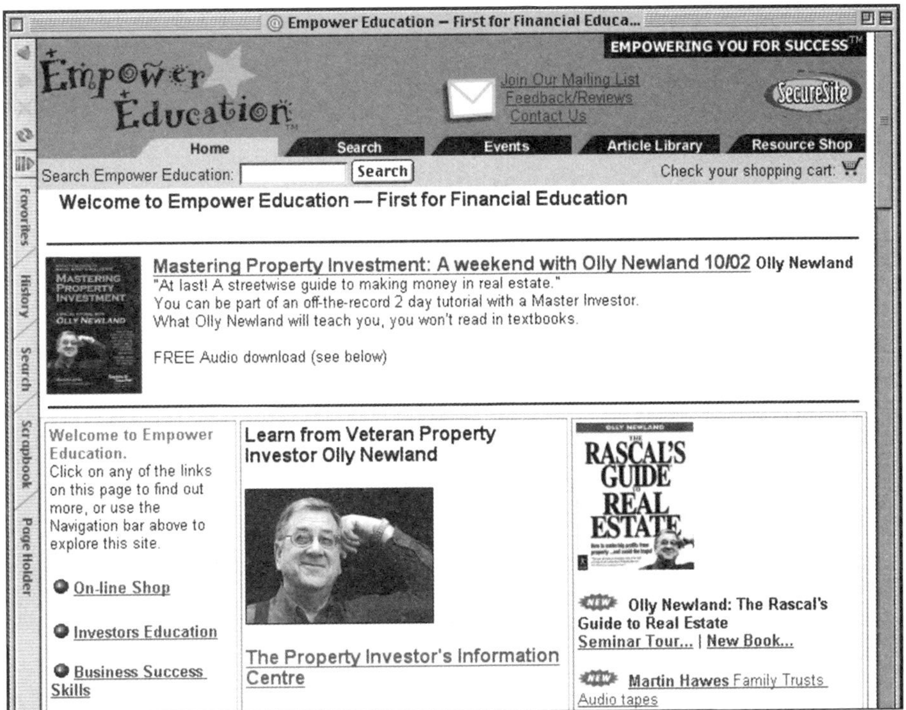
Empower Education – First for Financial Educa...

EMPOWERING YOU FOR SUCCESS™

Empower Education™

Join Our Mailing List
Feedback/Reviews
Contact Us

SecureSite

Home | Search | Events | Article Library | Resource Shop

Search Empower Education: [Search] Check your shopping cart:

Welcome to Empower Education — First for Financial Education

Mastering Property Investment: A weekend with Olly Newland 10/02 Olly Newland
"At last! A streetwise guide to making money in real estate."
You can be part of an off-the-record 2 day tutorial with a Master Investor.
What Olly Newland will teach you, you won't read in textbooks.

FREE Audio download (see below)

Welcome to Empower Education.
Click on any of the links on this page to find out more, or use the Navigation bar above to explore this site.

- On-line Shop
- Investors Education
- Business Success Skills

Learn from Veteran Property Investor Olly Newland

The Property Investor's Information Centre

THE RASCAL'S GUIDE TO REAL ESTATE

NEW Olly Newland: The Rascal's Guide to Real Estate
Seminar Tour... | New Book...

NEW Martin Hawes Family Trusts Audio tapes

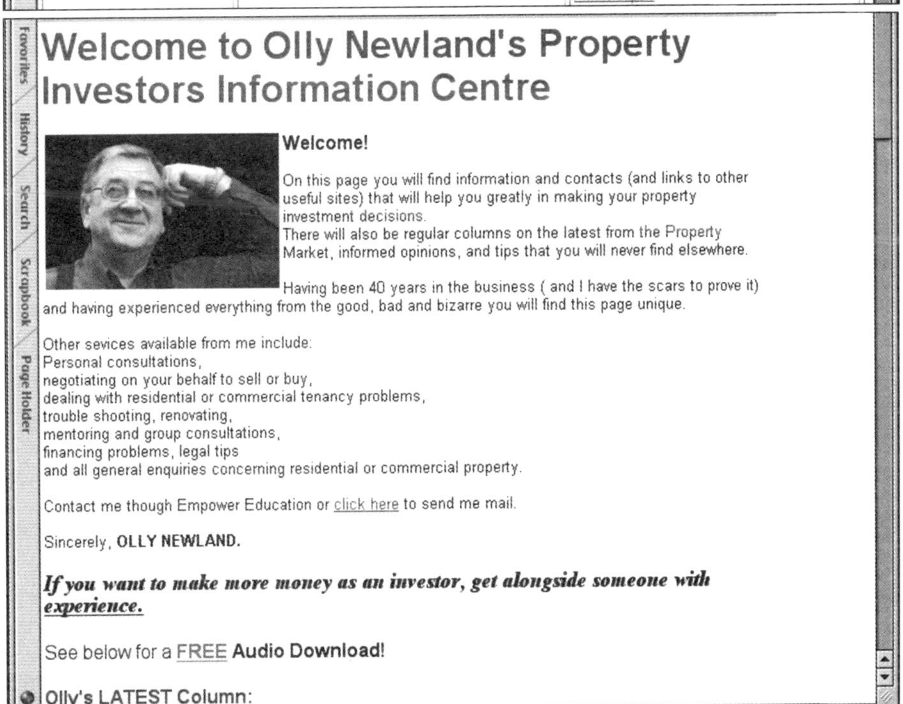
Welcome to Olly Newland's Property Investors Information Centre

Welcome!

On this page you will find information and contacts (and links to other useful sites) that will help you greatly in making your property investment decisions.
There will also be regular columns on the latest from the Property Market, informed opinions, and tips that you will never find elsewhere.

Having been 40 years in the business (and I have the scars to prove it) and having experienced everything from the good, bad and bizarre you will find this page unique.

Other sevices available from me include:
Personal consultations,
negotiating on your behalf to sell or buy,
dealing with residential or commercial tenancy problems,
trouble shooting, renovating,
mentoring and group consultations,
financing problems, legal tips
and all general enquiries concerning residential or commercial property.

Contact me though Empower Education or click here to send me mail.

Sincerely, **OLLY NEWLAND.**

If you want to make more money as an investor, get alongside someone with experience.

See below for a FREE **Audio Download!**

Olly's LATEST Column:

Index

S

T

V

W

Y